THE JOURNEY CONTINUES

הגדת פסח של מעין | The Ma'yan Passover Haggadah

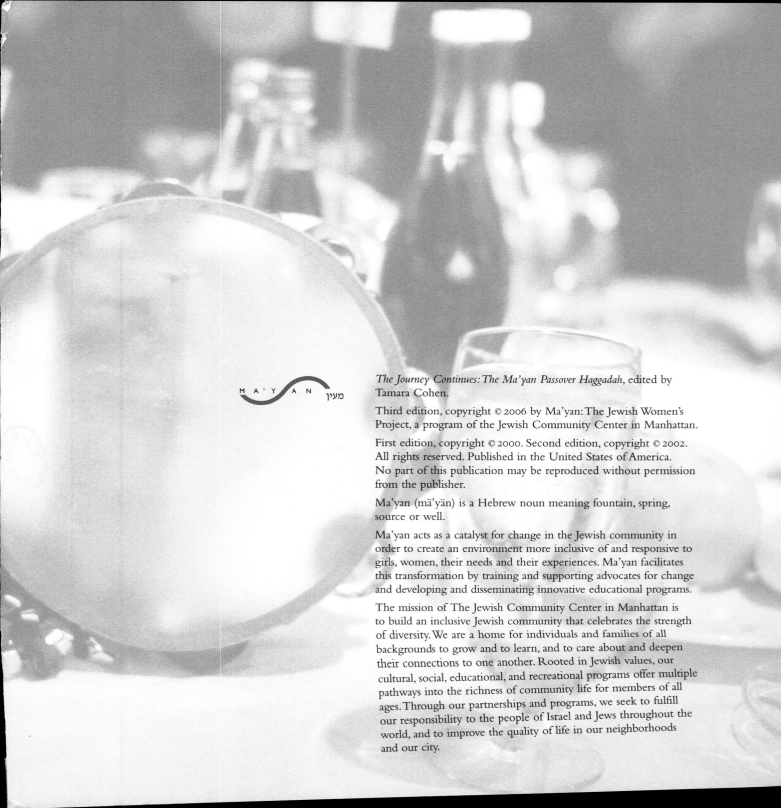

MA'YAN מעין

Ma'yan (mä'yän) is a Hebrew noun meaning fountain, spring,
source or well.

Ma'yan acts as a catalyst for change in the Jewish community in
order to create an environment more inclusive of and responsive to
girls, women, their needs and their experiences. Ma'yan facilitates
this transformation by training and supporting advocates for change
and developing and disseminating innovative educational programs.

The mission of The Jewish Community Center in Manhattan is
to build an inclusive Jewish community that celebrates the strength
of diversity. We are a home for individuals and families of all
backgrounds to grow and to learn, and to care about and deepen
their connections to one another. Rooted in Jewish values, our
cultural, social, educational, and recreational programs offer multiple
pathways into the richness of community life for members of all
ages. Through our partnerships and programs, we seek to fulfill
our responsibility to the people of Israel and Jews throughout the
world, and to improve the quality of life in our neighborhoods
and our city.

CONTENTS

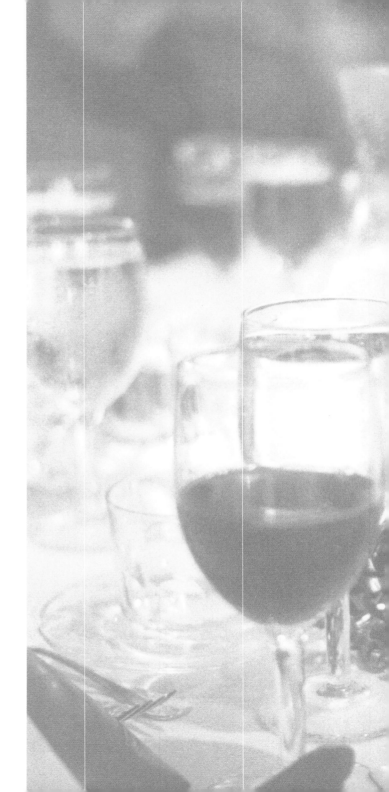

ACKNOWLEDGMENTS

In 1994, shortly after its founding, Ma'yan: The Jewish Women's Project of the Jewish Community Center in Manhattan held its first seder with over two hundred women and a few men in attendance. In New York the Ma'yan seders grew to include more than 2,000 participants a year, at four separate seders held on consecutive nights before Passover. At least 100 other community feminist seders using the Ma'yan Haggadah have been organized by groups of women throughout North America. In addition, the Haggadah has been translated into Hebrew and Russian and used in Israel and in sites across the CIS.

The Ma'yan Haggadah, originally written for our seders, is the product of the work of many hands, minds and hearts. Over the past six years it has been written and rewritten, edited and updated numerous times. Each new edition builds on the earlier versions as well as on feedback from seder participants. We acknowledge the tremendous work and creativity of each of the following people who have helped shape the text into its current form.

Ma'yan Haggadah, 1994 *Project Directors:* Rabbi Joy Levitt and Cantor Nancy Abramson. *Committee:* Tamara Cohen, Jennifer Cowan, Barbara Dobkin, Gila Gevirtz, Ronnie M. Horn, Debby Hirshman, Eve Landau, Wendy Lecker, Carol Levithan, Susan Oren, Judith Seed, Ruth Silverman, Nicki Tanner, Susan Schlechter, Susan Zuckerman.

Ma'yan Haggadah, 1995 *Editors:* Tamara Cohen, Rabbi Sue Levi Elwell, Ronnie M. Horn. *Committee:* Merle Feld, Rabbi Carol Levithan, Rabbi Joy Levitt.

Ma'yan Haggadah, 1996–1999 *Editors:* Tamara Cohen, Rabbi Sue Levi Elwell, Deborah Lynn Friedman, Ronnie M. Horn.

Ma'yan Haggadah, 2000 & 2002 *Editor:* Tamara Cohen. *Committee:* Barbara Dobkin, Erika Katske, Rabbi Jill Hammer, Eve Landau, Paulette Lipton, Susan Sapiro, Rabbi Rona Shapiro, Ruth Silverman. Updated 2006.

The Journey Continues is a celebration of Judaism at its best—inclusive, accessible, spiritually and intellectually challenging, and fully engaged in societal struggles for justice and meaning. Deeply committed to women's full integration in every aspect of Jewish life and practice, Ma'yan has created this Haggadah as a way of modeling the joy, strength and beauty that can result from Jewish feminists' ongoing relationship and struggle with tradition. *The Journey Continues* reflects our attempt to create a usable, lyrical document of integrity that invites new generations of women and men to celebrate "*z'man cheiruteinu*," our season of liberation.

This Haggadah is rooted in the belief that as more women discover the delight of preparing for and celebrating this holiday of journey and liberation, we reclaim an essential piece of our past and simultaneously assert our stake in the future. The Haggadah also enriches and renews Judaism by exposing men to the voices and experiences of women of the past and present.

Embedded in tradition and rooted in a commitment to a Judaism fully inclusive of women and men, the text integrates diverse approaches to Passover and the Exodus story. Some readings focus on the personal challenge of embracing freedom in our own lives; others approach the narrative of Passover as a metaphor for the experience of Jewish women throughout the ages and as an opportunity to articulate a vision of a world in which freedom belongs to all people.

Ma'yan's commitment to inclusivity is reflected in the Haggadah's accessibility to diverse audiences of Jews and non-Jews. All Hebrew is transliterated and translated. Directions that explain every step of the seder ritual are printed in color in the left column. Additional commentary, designated by large colored boxes, offers explanations of the meanings behind various actions and readings. These commentary boxes relate the innovations in this Haggadah to their counterparts in a traditional Haggadah.

The Journey Continues includes many songs written by contemporary composer Debbie Friedman. Singing the songs in this Haggadah will transform your seder experience and help participants connect with the text in a new way. All songs are printed as sung, in italics, to ease participation. A tape, CD, and songbook with full musical notation of most songs in this Haggadah are available through Sounds Write 1. 800. 9. sound. 9, or on the web at www.soundswrite.com.

Designed for home and communal settings, *The Journey Continues* can be used comfortably in gatherings of women and men, in multi-generational groups of family and friends, and in circles of women and girls. It can be used in its entirety or as a supplement to other *Haggadot* (plural). If you are planning to use this Haggadah for a communal seder, be sure to order Ma'yan's *Guide to Planning Communal Feminist Seders*, available free of charge on the web at www.mayan.org or through our office at 646. 505. 4432.

Seders[1] are not rituals led by experts. They are home-based, peer-led rituals that can help us revive our personal connections with Jewish history, and restore our sense of ownership of Judaism's future. We are told that each one of us personally left Egypt, and each of us must re-experience the Exodus, telling the story of our own freedom. When we truly do this—using our own voices, valuing our own insights, and building on the rich texts of our evolving tradition—we create inspirational seders and participate in the transformation of Judaism. Through this process, we can experience the blessing of being free to embrace the past as well as the future.

---

1 Given the general usage of seder as an English word we have chosen to use seders as the plural form of seder. However, it should be noted that the correct Hebrew plural for the word seder is *s'darim*.

A Brief History

The Haggadah is a collection of biblical excerpts and ritual directions, based upon the order for telling the story prescribed in the second-century *Mishnah*.[2] In the early centuries of the Common Era, *Haggadot* were not yet available as separate documents but were included in festival prayer books or legal works about Passover. It was not until the 7th or 8th century that *Haggadot* were first compiled as separate volumes. Since the 15th century, more than 2,700 editions of the Haggadah have been published.

While the Haggadah has been adapted by each generation and culture that has used it, the transformations of the Haggadah in the last decades of the 20th century have been truly remarkable in their scope, goals, and intended audiences. The earliest feminist *Haggadot* were born in the late 1960s and early 1970s, a time when seders were being held at anti-war rallies, during civil rights marches, and in lesbian feminist collectives. Some early feminist *Haggadot* changed the English text to include women and men, while others used the context of the seder to explore women's relationship with all of Jewish tradition.[3] Today, as women's seders are celebrated throughout the U.S. and Canada, new *Haggadot* are created every year. Many draw on existing texts and integrate them with original writings by members of local communities. Thus, this Haggadah takes its place on an ever-expanding shelf of diverse and creative *Haggadot,* each telling the story of the Exodus in its own unique voice.

---

2 The *Mishnah* is the legal codification containing the core of the Oral Law.

3 For a comprehensive exploration of the development and range of feminist *Haggadot*, see Maida E. Solomon, "Claiming Our Questions: Feminism and Judaism in Women's Haggadot" in Joyce Antler, ed. *Talking Back: Images of Jewish Women in American Popular Culture* (Hanover, N.H.: University Press of New England and Brandeis University Press, 1998). Both Ma'yan and the Jewish Women's Resource Center at the National Council of Jewish Women, New York Section, maintain collections of women's *Haggadot* that are available to the public.

Language Jews have always struggled with God; the name "Israel," in fact, can be understood to mean "God-wrestler." Feminists have always struggled both with religious tradition and with the nature and uses of power. So it is not surprising that central concerns of many Jewish feminists involve rethinking the way we talk about, imagine, and understand God and God's power. The questions raised by Jewish feminists and feminists of other religious traditions are in some ways very similar to thousand-year-old questions about the nature of Divine Being. On the other hand, the attention to issues of gender and hierarchy which are at the forefront of feminist re-visions of the Divine are unique to our era.

For centuries Jews have addressed God in formal prayer through exclusively masculine language. While the masculine language does not necessarily imply a male God, its constant and universal use has had the effect of gendering God as male. Thus, the use of feminine God-language in this Haggadah is intended to offer a balance, enabling us to name God as truly beyond gender and at the same time, as fully encompassing both femaleness and maleness.[4]

For some readers, the innovative God-language and imagery found in these pages will be unsettling. For others already comfortable in Jewish Renewal, Reconstructionist or other liberal streams of Judaism, the blessing formulations might not feel fluid enough. Regardless of where you stand on the continuums of fluidity, comfort and principle when it comes to blessings and God-language, you will be faced in this Haggadah with the opportunity to situate yourself in language that works for you. At the same time, you will be reminded that there is another way to express the blessing you are uttering.

Every blessing in this Haggadah is offered in three ways: two in Hebrew and one in English. The first is always the innovative formulation which retains the structure of the original blessing but alters language, gender and core imagery; the second blessing is

---

4 There is no option for gender-neutral language in Hebrew.

traditional. The English blessing is a literal translation of the innovative blessing that can also be understood as a creative translation of the traditional one. The innovative blessings used in this Haggadah have been written to sound and look very similar to the traditional blessings. This is meant to assist those less familiar with Hebrew and allow the concurrent use of both versions of the blessings by different people.

The innovative blessings begin with the same formulation as the traditional blessings, but they address God using a feminine verb form rather than a masculine one. The name of God that is used in these blessings is an ancient name for God, יָה *Yah*. This name is used in the familiar phrase הַלְלוּיָה *Halleluyah*, Praise God. יָה *Yah* is made up of the first two letters (or the first and last letter) of יהוה YHWH, the name of God known as the Tetragrammaton. According to tradition this name was only pronounced once a year, on *Yom Kippur*, by the High Priest in the Holy of Holies in the Temple. As there is no longer a Temple, the Tetragrammaton is no longer pronounced and has been replaced in prayer by the word *Adonai*, which means "my Lord."

While *Adonai* implies a masculine God who rules over us, יהוה YHWH can be understood as a name of God made up of all tenses of the verb "to be." This suggests a living God, a God that is Being itself. As God says at the burning bush "אֶהְיֶה אֲשֶׁר אֶהְיֶה" *"Eheyeh Asher Eheyeh,"* "I will be what I will be" (EXODUS 3:14). God as verb rather than subject, God as process, existence—these are new ways of thinking about God that are opened up through the use of יָה Yah. The alternative blessings include a further change. Instead of calling on God as מֶלֶךְ הָעוֹלָם *Melech Ha'olam*, King of the World, we invoke God's sovereignty through the term רוּחַ הָעוֹלָם *Ruach Ha'olam*, Spirit of the World. The image of God as a unifying force or spirit carries for many contemporary Jews the power that kingship must have carried for

the early rabbis. This Divine Spirit is first described in Genesis, before the creation of the world: וְרוּחַ אֱלֹהִים מְרַחֶפֶת עַל־פְּנֵי הַמָּיִם *V'ruach elohim m'rachefet al'pnei hamayim*, "God's spirit hovered over the face of the deep" (GENESIS 1:2). The word רוּחַ *Ruach* is conjugated as feminine and is an image associated with primordial creative power. רוּחַ *Ruach* also means wind and breath, two additional images that many people find useful in thinking about God.

A final note about the blessings. If you or members of your community are concerned about the permissibility (according to Jewish law) of reciting specific holiday blessings on a day that is not a holiday, we recommend the following: explain that according to the principle לְשֵׁם חִינוּךְ "*l'shem chinuch*," in the name of education, there is never a problem saying blessings and using God's name for the purpose of teaching. If you still find it personally uncomfortable to act as if it is Passover before the actual festival begins, skip the holiday blessings and use only the blessings or phrases appropriate for any time of the year.

The Four Cups

Aside from connecting the four cups to God's four reiterations of the promise to take the Israelites out of Egypt, the traditional Haggadah does not dwell on the symbolism of the four cups. In *The Journey Continues* the four cups are used to honor Jewish women leaders, teachers, and activists throughout history who worked to free others. The four cups will require some advance preparation on your part as you have a choice about which four women to honor. Not only can you choose from the 19 profiles included in Appendix 1, you can also write your own cup dedications, honoring women in your family or community. You can also read more profiles of Jewish women in history at www.jwa.org.

Readers	Seders work best when everyone participates. In this Haggadah every section that begins with the word "Readers" is intended for shared reading. These sections are further divided by thin colored lines which indicate when to switch readers. The "Readers" parts can also be read responsively, with, for example, different sections of the table or different age groups reading alternating paragraphs.
Tzedakah and Tikkun Olam	Part of what makes this Haggadah different is the way in which it insists on a connection between our wishes for a better, freer world and our power to make those wishes a reality. This Haggadah tries to bridge intention with action by including suggestions for *tzedakah*, giving money to increase justice, and for *tikkun olam*, repair of the world. Throughout the text in the "Do Something!" sections, you will find suggestions for concrete actions. Some will describe places to give money; others will suggest ideas for volunteer social service and advocacy projects. Appendix II contains complete contact information for every organization and project mentioned in the Haggadah as well as ways to find updated information about a wide array of institutions involved in *tikkun olam* work.

Read through the Haggadah in the weeks before your seder and decide how you want to use *The Journey Continues*. Think about how to "customize" a seder experience that will work for the group you are gathering. Invite your guests to bring something to share: a question, a recipe, or a poem to contribute to the evening. Think about dividing leadership responsibilities for different parts of the seder. If you plan to hold or attend more than one seder, you have the flexibility of doing each one differently. You might hold a more traditional seder on one night and a more explicitly feminist seder on another.

For some people seders can be complicated balancing acts—between family and friends; between the needs of children, teens, adults and older adults; between various relationships to tradition, ritual and change. It is helpful to remember that change is gradual. Even if you focus on adding just one new element or feminist reading to your seder each year, you will discover that over time, as you take the steps to transform your seders, you will be continually inspired and transformed.

The Seder Table

The seder table is the central physical space around which the seder unfolds. Even if you choose to hold part of your seder away from the table in a more comfortable space, your table should reflect the festivity and sanctity of the holiday. Crowded with dishes, glasses, bottles of wine and grape juice, flowers (not too high), and *Haggadot*, the table must also have room for the following:

Matzah

You need enough matzah for everyone to eat and three ceremonial *matzot* (plural) to be placed somewhere near the center of the table in a large napkin or special matzah holder. If your seder is held before Passover, you might want to use egg matzah so that you can save "the real thing" for Passover. Some people use *sh'murah matzah* for the three ceremonial *matzot*. These *matzot* are hand-made from wheat that has been watched from the time it was harvested.

A traditional seder plate includes five or six symbolic foods: *karpas, maror, z'roa, beitzah, charoset* and sometimes *chazeret.*

Karpas can be any vegetable for which the blessing over fruit of the earth is recited. Parsley or another green leafy vegetable is traditionally used. Jews of Eastern European descent sometimes use potatoes as they were the closest to a green vegetable available during Passover.

For *maror*, bitter herbs, use horseradish root or bitter lettuce. Put enough on the seder plate for everyone, as the *maror* will be eaten during the seder.

The *z'roa*, shank bone, is a reminder of the Passover sacrifice. According to the Talmud vegetarians may substitute a raw beet, which also bleeds when cut (TRACTATE PESACHIM 114B). The *z'roa* is not eaten at the seder.

The *beitzah* is a roasted hard-boiled egg. It is included on the seder plate in remembrance of the holiday sacrifice offered at the Temple. It can also be seen as a symbol of creation and the cycle of life and death, as eggs are eaten by mourners after a funeral. While the *beitzah* on the seder plate is not eaten or used during the seder, some people serve hard-boiled eggs and salt water before the meal.

The *charoset*, a mixture of wine, fruits, nuts, and spices, symbolizes the mortar with which the Israelites made bricks during slavery. Ashkenazi *charoset* is usually made of apples, nuts, sweet wine, honey or sugar, and cinnamon. Sephardic *charoset* recipes contain dates, figs, apricots, almonds, and less or no wine. Make plenty of *charoset* as it is always a favorite.

The sixth and optional item on the seder plate is *chazeret*, a second bitter herb, which is added to the Hillel sandwich. You can use romaine lettuce or prepared horseradish for *chazeret*.

While all seder tables should include at least one central seder plate, some people prepare individual seder plates for each person. These plates should have all the ritual foods that will be eaten during the seder, but they do not have to include the *beitzah* or the *z'roa*.

The Orange	In the early 1980s, while speaking at Oberlin College Hillel, Jewish feminist scholar Dr. Susannah Heschel was introduced to an early feminist Haggadah that contained a story in which an *hasidic* rebbe tells a young Jewish lesbian that there's as much room for a lesbian in Judaism as there is for a crust of bread on the Seder plate. Heschel felt that to put bread on the *seder* plate would be to accept that Jewish lesbians and gay men violate Judaism like *chametz* violates Passover. So, at her next seder, she chose an orange as a symbol of inclusion of gays and lesbians and others who are marginalized within the Jewish community. She offered the orange as a symbol of the fruitfulness for all Jews when lesbians and gay men are contributing and active members of Jewish life. In addition, each orange segment had a few seeds that had to be spit out — a gesture of spitting out, repudiating the homophobia of Judaism. When lecturing, Heschel often mentioned her custom as one of many new feminist rituals that have been developed in the last twenty years. She writes, "Somehow, though, the typical patriarchal maneuver occurred: My idea of an orange and my intention of affirming lesbians and gay men were transformed. Now the story circulates that a MAN said to me that a woman belongs on the *bimah* as an orange on the seder plate. A woman's words are attributed to a man, and the affirmation of lesbians and gay men is simply erased. Isn't that precisely what's happened over the centuries to women's ideas?"[5]
Elijah's Cup	Place an Elijah's Cup at the center of the table. The cup should look different from all other cups on the table. Fill the cup with wine at the beginning of the seder or leave the cup empty for most of the seder and fill it before singing *Eiliyahu Hanavi.* The Prophet Elijah participates symbolically in many Jewish rituals. According to tradition, Elijah will herald the coming of the Messianic Age. The subject of many folk legends and magical tales, he is said to be wandering the earth in the disguise of a beggar, monitoring our treatment of the poor and disadvantaged.

5 Susannah Heschel, "The Definitive Orange on the Seder Plate Story," E-mail. 5 Apr. 2001.

Miriam's Cup	A Miriam's Cup is a new ritual object that is placed on the seder table beside the Cup of Elijah. Miriam's Cup is filled with water close to the beginning of the seder. It serves as a symbol of Miriam's Well, the source of water for the Israelites in the desert. There are many legends about Miriam's Well. It is said to have been a magical source of water that followed the Israelites for forty years because of the merit of Miriam. The waters of this well were said to be healing and sustaining waters. Thus Miriam's Cup can be seen as a symbol of all that sustains us through our journeys, while Elijah's Cup is seen as a symbol of a future Messianic time. Miriam's Cup can be used in other rituals throughout the year. The cup images throughout the Haggadah are Miriam's Cups from Ma'yan's 1997 exhibition "Drawing from the Source: Miriam, Women's Creativity and New Ritual." For more information, contact Ma'yan.
Tambourine	Include tambourines on your table to offer children as well as adults an additional way to rejoice and participate. The instrument is deeply connected to the story of the Exodus as it was used by Miriam and the Israelite women when they danced and sang at the shores of the Red Sea after having successfully left Egypt and escaped the Egyptian army. According to Dr. Lori Lefkovitz, "In ancient Israel, a woman's timbrel was as important to her as Shabbat candlesticks are today." As it says,

וַתִּקַּח מִרְיָם הַנְּבִיאָה אֲחוֹת אַהֲרֹן
אֶת-הַתֹּף בְּיָדָהּ וַתֵּצֶאןָ כָל-הַנָּשִׁים
אַחֲרֶיהָ בְּתֻפִּים וּבִמְחֹלֹת:

"And Miriam the prophetess, the sister of Aaron, took
a timbrel in her hand; and all the women went out
after her with timbrels, dancing" (EXODUS 15:20).

Tzedakah Box	Ma'yan's communal seders include a *tzedakah* box on each table. Every year we collect *tzedakah* during the seder and donate it to an organization or cause linked to Jewish women. This is another way of bridging our liturgy with action. If your seder is being held during Passover itself and you do not handle money on festivals (for Jewish legal reasons), we suggest that you put the *tzedakah* box near your candles and collect money before you light candles on the first night. Otherwise, consider including this ritual object on the table at your home seders next to the Miriam and Elijah Cups. It will provoke new questions whose answers can connect the value of *tzedakah* to the visions of healing and redemption symbolized by the Miriam and Elijah Cups. *Tzedakah* can be given during any of the "Do Something!" sections of this Haggadah.
Additional Items	Candlesticks and candles; a bowl with salt water for dipping the *karpas*; a pitcher of water and a bowl for hand-washing; hard-boiled eggs to eat before the meal (optional); pillows for sitting comfortably like free people; a plate of scallions reminiscent of the onions that sustained the Israelites in Egypt (NUMBERS 11:5) and the whips of the Egyptian taskmasters. (The scallions are used by Iranian Jews during the *Dayeinu* in a playful reenactment of the taskmaster's whipping.)

בדיקת חמץ B'DIKAT CHAMEITZ SEARCHING FOR LEAVEN

COMMENTARY

Traditional preparation for Passover involves a thorough cleaning of everything you own: your house, your car, the pockets of your coats and jackets, your office space, etc. All of these areas are to be free of *chameitz*, leaven, by the morning of the first Passover seder. Some contemporary Jews clean only their kitchens, while others simply refrain from eating bread products during Passover.

The original prohibition of leaven on Passover comes from Exodus: "Seven days you shall eat unleavened bread...you shall remove leaven from your houses" (EXODUS 12:15).

If you dispose of your *chameitz* before Passover, plan to donate it to a food bank in fulfillment of the *mitzvah* of *ma'ot chittin*, caring for the hungry.

B'dikat Chameitz is a ritual traditionally conducted the night before the first seder. The ritual is a dramatic representation of the care with which we undertake preparation for Passover. To perform the ritual, hide ten pieces of *chameitz* in your home and then search for them with the light of a candle. Gather together the *chameitz* with a feather and a wooden spoon. Before beginning your search, say:

בְּרוּכָה אַתְּ יָהּ אֱלֹהֵינוּ רוּחַ הָעוֹלָם
אֲשֶׁר קִדְּשַׁתְנוּ בְּמִצְוֹתֶיהָ וְצִוַּתְנוּ
עַל בְּעוּר חָמֵץ.

B'rucha at yah eloheinu ruach ha'olam
asher kid'shatnu b'mitzvoteha v'tzivatnu
al biur chameitz.

or

בָּרוּךְ אַתָּה יְיָ אֱלֹהֵינוּ מֶלֶךְ הָעוֹלָם
אֲשֶׁר קִדְּשָׁנוּ בְּמִצְוֹתָיו וְצִוָּנוּ
עַל בְּעוּר חָמֵץ.

Baruch atah adonai eloheinu melech ha'olam
asher kid'shanu b'mitzvotav v'tzivanu
al biur chameitz.

You are Blessed, O God, Spirit of the World, who makes us holy with *mitzvot* and commands us to burn *chameitz*.

After the search, recite the following Aramaic formulation.

כָּל חֲמִירָא וַחֲמִיעָא דְּאִכָּא בִרְשׁוּתִי.
דַּחֲמִיתֵהּ וּדְלָא חֲמִיתֵהּ.
דְּבִעַרְתֵּהּ וּדְלָא בִעַרְתֵּהּ.
לִבָּטֵל וְלֶהֱוֵי הֶפְקֵר כְּעַפְרָא דְּאַרְעָא:

Kol chamira vachami'a d'ika virshuti.
Dachamitei u'd'la chamitei.
D'viartei u'd'la viartei.
Libateil v'lehevei hefker k'afra d'ara.

Every sort of *chameitz* in my possession, which I have seen or not seen, destroyed or not destroyed, let it be null and void, ownerless, like the dust of the earth.

It is traditional to set aside the *chameitz* you have found and burn it the next morning. The Aramaic formulation above is repeated after the burning.

הסדר | haseder   the seder

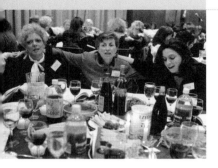

COMMENTARY

In our era, we have begun to prepare for Passover with a new ritual—
a women's seder. For one evening before Passover we sit together, dance,
study, sing and tell stories of our own liberation. In this way we ready
ourselves for the upcoming celebration of freedom.

READERS

Why is this night different from all other nights?

On this night, we gather together to prepare
for Passover, outside of our kitchens, in a way our
foremothers could have never imagined.

On this night we join as a community to rid
ourselves of a different kind of *chameitz*.

What do we cleanse ourselves of tonight?

The exhaustion of cleaning and cooking.

The echo of exclusionary language.

The weight of history.

The fear of women's voices.

The silencing of women's stories.

The violence done to women's bodies.

The pressure to conform to one image of who
Jewish women are supposed to be.

The lingering belief that this tradition doesn't
belong to women.

Let us gather all this together like crumbs. Like *chameitz* we are ready to burn. Let us enter into this seder as if there were no more *chameitz* anywhere.

As if God had forever delighted in the image of Herself in each and every one of us.

As if freedom had been ours always, fully—like an open sea.

כָּל חֲמִירָא וַחֲמִיעָא . . .

Kol chamira vachami'a...
Every sort of *chameitz*...

לִבָּטֵל וְלֶהֱוֵי הֶפְקֵר כְּעַפְרָא דְאַרְעָא.

Libateil v'lehevei hefkeir k'afra d'ara.
...Let it be null and void, ownerless, like the dust of the earth.

You may choose to actually burn some bread crumbs to complete this ritual.

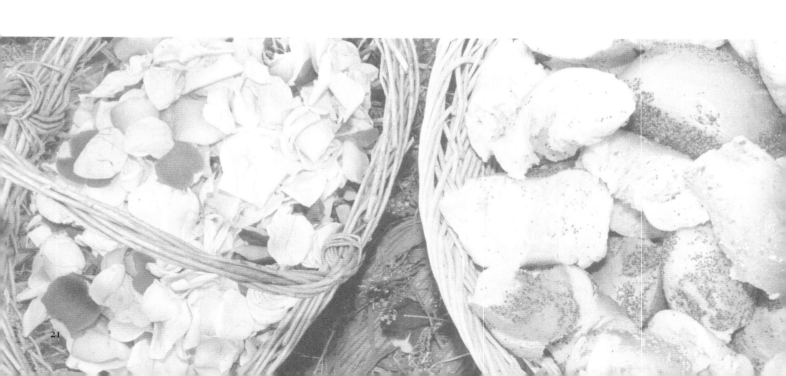

ברוכות הבאות | B'RUCHOT HABAOT

בְּרוּכוֹת הַבָּאוֹת תַּחַת כַּנְפֵי הַשְּׁכִינָה
בְּרוּכִים הַבָּאִים תַּחַת כַּנְפֵי הַשְּׁכִינָה

B'ruchot habaot tachat kanfei hash'chinah
B'ruchim habaim tachat kanfei hash'chinah

May you be blessed beneath the wings of Sh'chinah
Be blessed with love, be blessed with peace.

Introduce yourself to the others at the table by tracing your matrilineage using the following formulation:

for females: I am _____ *bat* (daughter of) _____ *bat* _____ *bat* _____

for males: I am _____ *ben* (son of) _____ *ben* _____ *ben* _____

Use your English, Hebrew, Yiddish and/or Ladino names. Go back as many generations as you can. You may choose to invoke the names of women who have been like mothers and grandmothers for you regardless of biological ties.

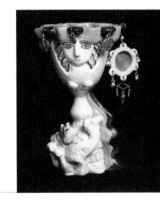

COMMENTARY

Sh'chinah, a feminine Hebrew noun, is a traditional name for the Divine Presence. It has been understood as the imminent aspect of God that dwells among the people of Israel. In mystical texts the *Sh'chinah* is a feminine manifestation of God imagined as having a traditionally gendered relationship with the masculine, more active aspect of God. More recently, *Sh'chinah* has been reappropriated by feminists in search of a traditional feminine image of the Divine.

The time is now.
We've gathered 'round.
So bring all your gifts,
And bring all your burdens with you.

No need to hide.
Arms open wide.
We gather as one.
To make a makom kadosh.

We come to tell.
We come to hear.
We come to teach, to learn,
We come to grow.
And so we say,

The time is now.
Sing to the One.
God's Presence is here,
Sh'chinah, You will dwell among us.

We'll make this space
A holy place,
So separate, so whole,
Rejoice every soul
Who enters here.

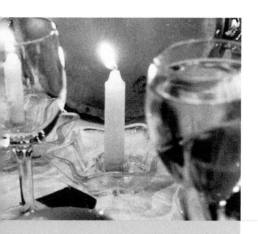

COMMENTARY

A *makom kadosh* is a holy place. *Hamakom* (lit., the place) is an ancient name for God. *Kadosh* (lit., holy) carries the implication of something set apart and separate. Any place can be set aside as holy through the actions of the people who inhabit it. Thus the purpose of this song is to help facilitate a transition in atmosphere by inviting seder participants to experience themselves as entering a separate space in time, a space with the potential for holiness. Whether your seder is being held in a gymnasium, a dining room, or a rented hall, it can now become a sanctuary, a *makom kadosh*.

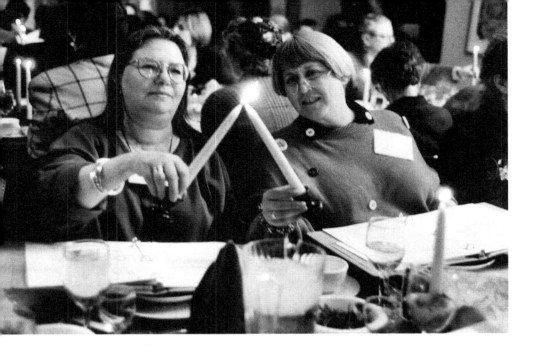

This song, based on a *techine* for lighting candles, can be sung before, during, or after lighting the candles.

LIGHT THESE LIGHTS

O hear my prayer,
I sing to You.
Be gracious to the ones I love,
And bless them with goodness,
and mercy and peace,
O hear my prayer to You.

Let us light these lights
And see the way to You,
And let us say: Amen.

Techines are Yiddish prayers, some of which were written by women between the sixteenth and nineteenth centuries in Eastern and Central Europe. *Techines* (from the Hebrew word *le'hit'chanen*, to supplicate) were used by women for prayer at home or in the synagogue. They often refer to specific women's commandments like candlelighting and contain references to the Matriarchs and other biblical women.

Light the candles and recite the blessings.
Add the words in parentheses on Shabbat.

Candlelighting using feminine God-language

בְּרוּכָה אַתְּ יָהּ
אֱלֹהֵינוּ רוּחַ הָעוֹלָם
אֲשֶׁר קִדְּשַׁתְנוּ בְּמִצְוֹתֶיהָ וְצִוַּתְנוּ
לְהַדְלִיק נֵר שֶׁל (שַׁבָּת וְשֶׁל) יוֹם טוֹב:

B'rucha at yah
eloheinu ruach ha'olam
asher kid'shatnu b'mitzvoteha v'tzivatnu
l'hadlik neir shel (shabbat v'shel) yom tov.

You are Blessed, Our God, Spirit of the World,
who makes us holy with *mitzvot* and
commands us to kindle the light of
(Shabbat and of) the festival day.

בְּרוּכָה אַתְּ יָהּ
אֱלֹהֵינוּ רוּחַ הָעוֹלָם
שֶׁהֶחֱיָתְנוּ וְקִיְּמַתְנוּ וְהִגִּיעַתְנוּ
לַזְּמַן הַזֶּה:

B'rucha at yah
eloheinu ruach ha'olam
shehecheyatnu v'kiy'matnu v'higiatnu
laz'man hazeh.

You are Blessed, Our God, Spirit of the World,
who keeps us in life, who sustains us,
and who enables us to reach this season.

Candlelighting using traditional God-language

בָּרוּךְ אַתָּה יְיָ
אֱלֹהֵינוּ מֶלֶךְ הָעוֹלָם
אֲשֶׁר קִדְּשָׁנוּ בְּמִצְוֹתָיו וְצִוָּנוּ
לְהַדְלִיק נֵר שֶׁל (שַׁבָּת וְשֶׁל) יוֹם טוֹב:

Baruch atah adonai
eloheinu melech ha'olam
asher kid'shanu b'mitzvotav v'tzivanu
l'hadlik neir shel (shabbat v'shel) yom tov.

You are Blessed, Our God, Spirit of the World, who makes us holy with *mitzvot* and commands us to kindle the light of (Shabbat and of) the festival day.

בָּרוּךְ אַתָּה יְיָ
אֱלֹהֵינוּ מֶלֶךְ הָעוֹלָם
שֶׁהֶחֱיָנוּ וְקִיְּמָנוּ וְהִגִּיעָנוּ
לַזְּמַן הַזֶּה:

Baruch atah adonai
eloheinu melech ha'olam
shehecheyanu v'kiy'manu v'higianu
laz'man hazeh.

You are Blessed, Our God, Spirit of the World, who keeps us in life, who sustains us, and who enables us to reach this season.

Alternative or additional candlelighting blessing for women's seders

מַה טֹּבוּ סְדָרֵינוּ בְּנוֹת יִשְׂרָאֵל
כְּאוֹר חָדָשׁ הַמֵּאִיר עוֹלָם:

Ma tovu sidreinu b'not yisra'el,
k'or chadash ha'me'ir olam.

Women of Israel, the wonder of our seders brings new light to the world.

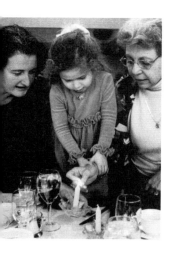

For centuries Jewish women have followed the blessing of the festival lights with a *techine*, a private petitionary prayer. Tonight we keep this tradition alive with the words of this adapted Sephardic woman's prayer:

יְהִי רָצוֹן מִלְּפָנֶיךָ

יָהּ אֱלֹהַי וֵאלֹהֵי אֲבוֹתַי וְאִמּוֹתַי

שֶׁתָּחֹנִי אוֹתִי וְאֶת מִשְׁפַּחְתִּי

וְתִתְּנִי לָנוּ וּלְכָל יִשְׂרָאֵל

חַיִּים טוֹבִים וַאֲרֻכִּים

וְתִזְכְּרִינוּ בְּזִכָּרוֹן טוֹב וּבִבְרָכָה

וְתִפְקְדִינוּ בִּפְקֻדַּת יְשׁוּעָה וְרַחֲמִים

וּתְבָרְכִינוּ בְּרָכוֹת גְּדוֹלוֹת

וְתַחְזִיקִי בָּתֵּינוּ.

Y'hi ratzon milfanayich,

yah elohai veilohei avotai v'imotai

shetachoni oti v'et mishpachti

v'tit'ni lanu ul'chol yisraeil

chayim tovim va'arukim

v'tizk'rinu b'zikaron tov uviv'racha

v'tifk'dinu bif'kudat y'shua v'rachamim

u't'varchinu b'rachot g'dolot

v'tachziki bateinu.

May it be Your will, my God and God of my ancestors, to be gracious to me and to all my family and to give us, and all Israel, a good and long life. Remember us with goodness and blessing, and grant us salvation and mercy. Grant us abundant blessing, and fortify the places we call home.

וְתַשְׁכִּינִי שְׁכִינָתֵךְ בֵּינֵינוּ

בְּהֵאָסְפוּתֵינוּ כַּאן הָעֶרֶב.

וּתְזַכֵּנוּ לְגַדֵּל

יְלָדִים חֲכָמִים וּנְבוֹנִים

אוֹהֲבֵי יָהּ יִרְאֵי אֱלֹהִים

אַנְשֵׁי אֱמֶת וּמְפִיצֵי קֹדֶשׁ.

מִי יִתֵּן וְתַלְמִידֵינוּ

יָאִירוּ אֶת־הָעוֹלָם

בַּתּוֹרָה וּבְמַעֲשִׂים טוֹבִים.

V'tashkini sh'chinateich beineinu

b'hei'asfuteinu kan ha'erev.

Ut'zakeinu l'gadeil

y'ladim chachamim un'vonim,

ohavei yah, yirei elohim,

anshei emet, um'fitzei kodesh.

Mi yitein v'talmideinu

ya'iru et ha'olam

batorah u'v'ma'asim tovim.

May Your Presence dwell among us as we gather here tonight. May we be blessed with wise and learned disciples and children, lovers of God who stand in awe of You, people who speak truth and spread holiness. May those we nurture light the world with Torah and good deeds.

שִׁמְעִי אֶת־תְּחִנָתִי בָּעֵת הַזֹּאת	Shim'i et t'chinati ba'eit hazot
בִּזְכוּת שָׂרָה וְרִבְקָה וְרָחֵל וְלֵאָה	bizchut sara v'rivka v'racheil v'lei'a,
וּבִלְהָה וְזִלְפָּה אִמּוֹתֵינוּ	v'bilha v'zilpa, imoteinu,
וְהָאִירִי אוֹר פָּנַיִךְ	v'ha'iri or panayich
לְעוֹלָם וָעֶד	l'olam va'ed,
בְּאוֹר נֵרוֹתֵינוּ וְנִוָּשֵׁעָה.	b'or neiroteinu v'nivashei'a.
וְנֹאמַר אָמֵן.	V'nomar amen.

Hear the prayers I utter now in the name of our mothers Sarah, Rebekah, Rachel, Leah, Bilhah and Zilpah. May Your light, reflected in these candles, surround us always. And let us say, Amen.

COMMENTARY

This prayer honors the mothers of all the children of Israel, including Bilhah and Zilpah, the maidservants of Rachel and Leah.

COMMENTARY

Beginning the seder with Miriam's Cup establishes yours as a seder that will consistently highlight women's roles in the Exodus. By involving every seder participant in the filling of Miriam's Cup, the participatory nature of the seder is also immediately established. Just as everyone has poured some water into Miriam's Cup, so, too, the presence of each person at the table will add something unique to the seder. On another level, when the Miriam's Cup is filled with water from each person's glass, we are enacting our hope of refilling the magical healing Well of Miriam through inclusiveness and collectivity.

Pass around the empty Miriam's Cup. Each person should pour some water from her or his own drinking glass, or from a pitcher of water, into the cup.

ALL

We begin our seder with כּוֹס מִרְיָם *kos miryam*, Miriam's Cup. Legend tells of a mysterious well filled with מַיִם חַיִּים *mayim hayyim*, living waters, that followed the Israelites through their wandering in the desert while Miriam was alive.

READERS

Miriam's Well was said to hold Divine power to heal and renew. Its fresh waters sustained our people as we were transformed from a generation shaped by slavery into a free nation. Throughout our subsequent journeys, we have sought to rediscover these living waters.

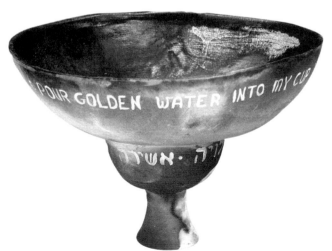

29

Tonight at our seder, let us remember that we are still on the journey. Just as the Holy One delivered Miriam and her people, just as they were sustained in the desert and transformed into a new people, so may we be delivered, sustained and transformed on our journey to a stronger sense of ourselves, both as individuals and as one people.

ALL

זֹאת כּוֹס מִרְיָם כּוֹס מַיִם חַיִּים
זֵכֶר לִיצִיאַת מִצְרָיִם:

Zot kos miryam, kos mayim chayyim.

Zeicher litzi'at mitzrayim.

This is the Cup of Miriam, the cup of living waters. Let us remember the Exodus from Egypt.

These are the living waters, God's gift to Miriam, which gave new life to Israel as we struggled in the wilderness. May the Cup of Miriam refresh and inspire us as we embark on our journey through the Haggadah.

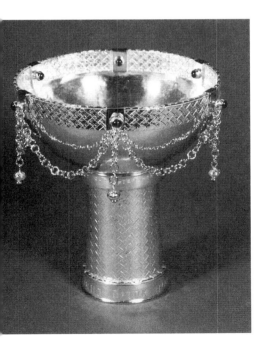

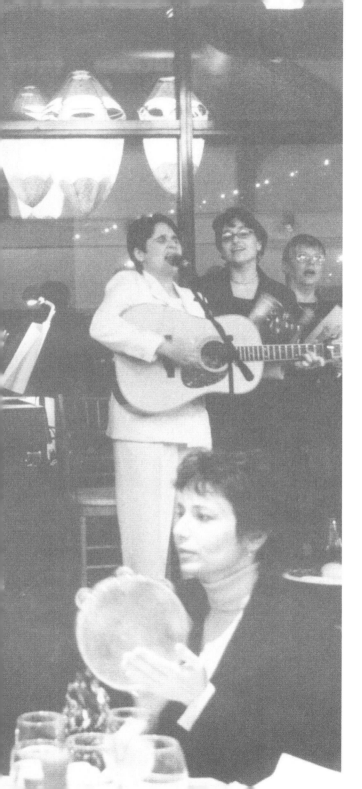

THE JOURNEY SONG

Where does the journey begin?
Where will we go?
Hours pass, the answers might change
As we keep moving along.

Stand at the shores of the sea
Fearful, we want to turn back.
The sea parts, our eyes fill with wonder
As we go along on our journey.

Where does the journey begin?
Where will we go?
Days pass, the answers can change
As we keep moving along.

Stepping into the unknown
Hear the echoes of Miriam's song
We awaken, retelling our stories
As we go along on our journey.

Where does the journey begin?
Where will we go?
Years pass, the answers have changed
As we keep moving along.

Cross the sea, it's the time
To sing a song, we are free
Dance with your timbrels in hand
There's no turning back from this journey.

Where does the journey begin?
Where will we go?
Hours pass, the answers might change
As we keep moving along.

Days pass, the answers can change
As we keep moving along
Years pass, the answers have changed
As we keep moving along.

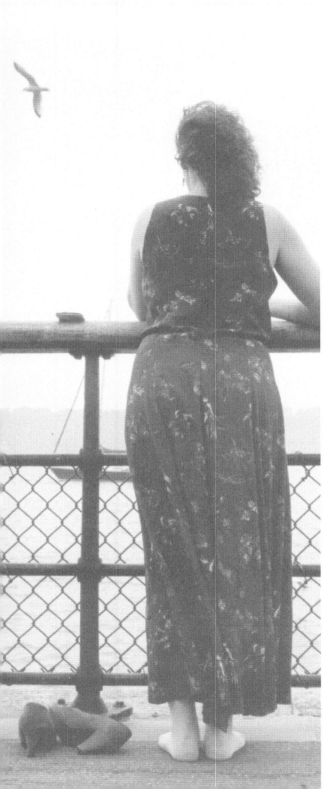

How does the journey to freedom begin?

Once, and then again and again. We wake and for the hundredth morning in a row grope in the early silence for the words to describe what is wrong. One day, words begin. We are wrenched from the patterns that have defined our lives. We can no longer live as we have lived.

How does our people's journey begin?

In the hut where the Israelite midwives work, Shifra turns to Pu'ah and sees in the spark of her partner's eye something she did not see the day before. Together they dare to defy Pharaoh, preserve life, ensure their people's future.

In the dark room where Yocheved labors to give birth, her daughter Miriam sits close by, humming a chant her grandmothers sang while mixing mortar. Suddenly she hears an infant's cry. And within her, hope rises like a new song. She sees beyond Egypt, to bright desert spaces and mountains, to far-off vineyards heavy with fruit.

How does the journey to freedom begin?

Once, and then again. In small, scattered, heroic acts and moments of vision until the humming rises and disparate voices come together into the cry of a people. "A long time after that the king of Egypt died, but the Israelites were still groaning under bondage, and their cry for help from the bondage rose up to God" (EXODUS 2:23).

32

Using the tune of *The Journey Song*, sing the order of the seder in Hebrew. This list functions as a mnemonic device to ease memorization of the key elements of the text.

THE ORDER

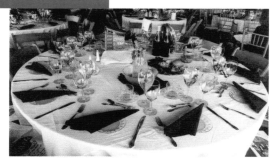

קַדֵּשׁ	**Kadeish**
וּרְחַץ	**Urchatz**
כַּרְפַּס	**Karpas**
יַחַץ	**Yachatz**
מַגִּיד	**Maggid**
רָחְצָה	**Rachtzah**
מוֹצִיא־מַצָּה	**Motzi Matzah**
מָרוֹר	**Maror**
כּוֹרֵךְ	**Koreich**
שֻׁלְחָן עוֹרֵךְ	**Shulchan Oreich**
צָפוּן	**Tzafun**
בָּרֵךְ	**Bareich**
הַלֵּל	**Hallel**
נִרְצָה	**Nirtzah**

Make Holy, Wash, Fruit of the Earth, Breaking the Middle Matzah, Telling the Story, Second Hand-Washing, Matzah Blessings, Bitter Herbs, Hillel Sandwich, The Festive Meal, Retrieving the Hidden Matzah, Blessing After the Meal, Songs of Praise, Concluding the Seder

קדש | kadeish   make holy

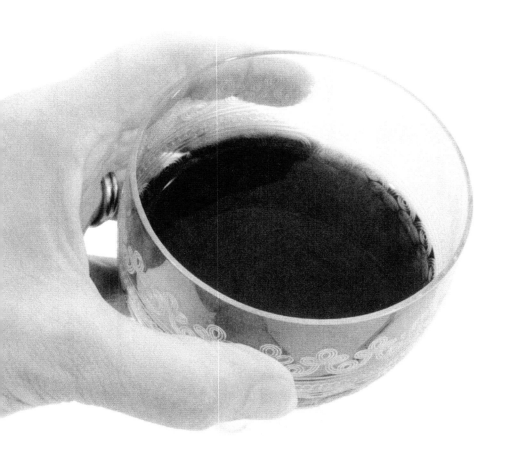

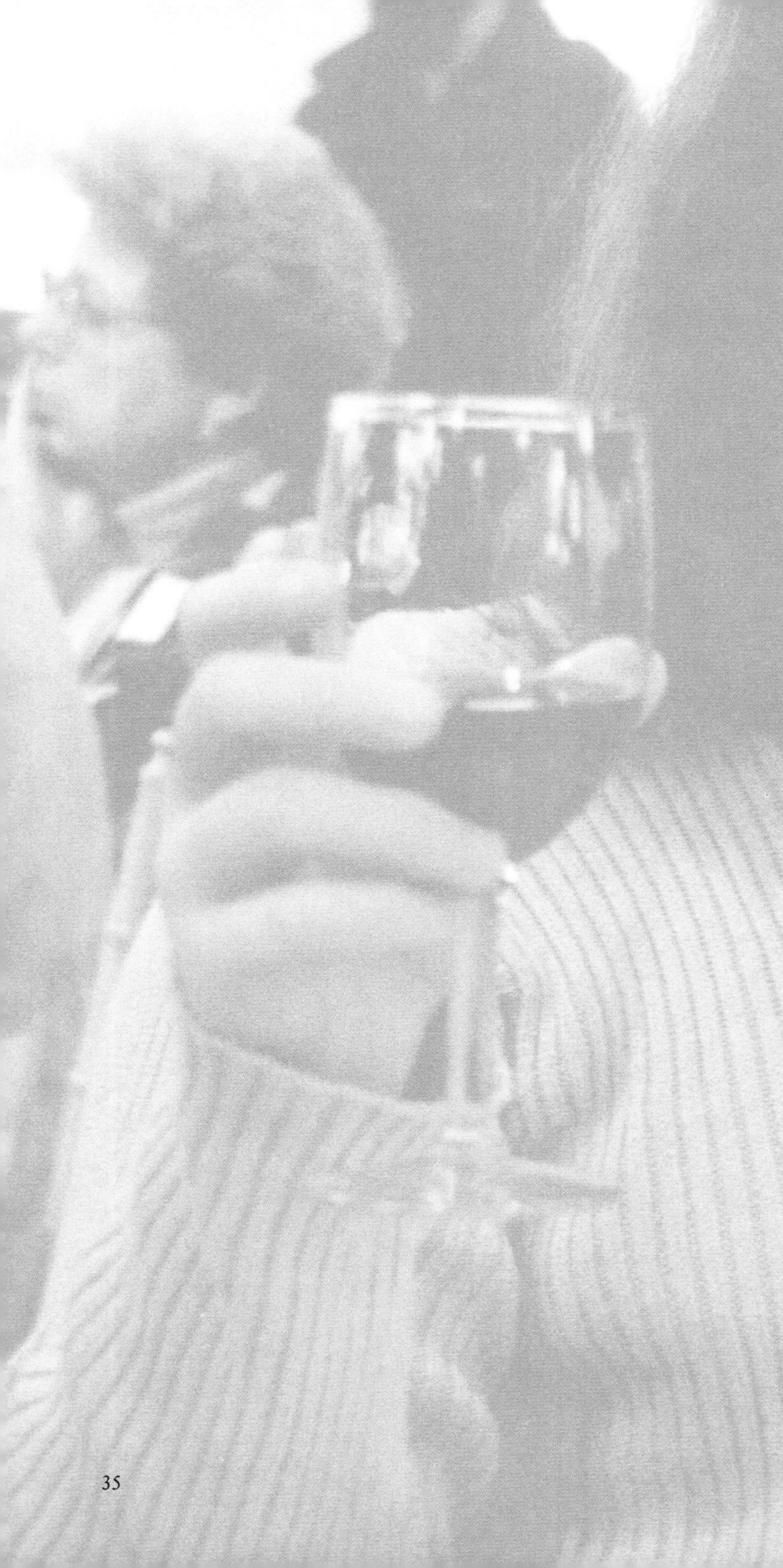

Tonight we will drink four cups of wine, traditionally linked to God's four promises to Israel.

ALL

As it is written, "I will bring you out from under the burdens of Egypt. I will deliver you from bondage. I will redeem you with an outstretched arm and great judgments. I will take you to be my people and I will be your God" (EXODUS 6:6-7).

READERS

In this seder the four cups of wine are also linked to historical and living Jewish women, who in their own eras have acted as God's partners in fulfilling the divine promises of redemption and freedom.

ALL

As it is written "It was for the sake of the righteous women of that generation that we were redeemed from Egypt" (BABYLONIAN TALMUD, SOTAH 9B).

Fill your first cup with wine or grape juice.

וְהוֹצֵאתִי אֶתְכֶם מִתַּחַת סִבְלֹת מִצְרָיִם: ...

V'hotzeiti etchem mitachat sivlot mitzrayim.

"...I will bring you out from under the burdens of Egypt" (EXODUS 6:6).

The first cup we drink tonight is linked to the verse from Exodus which tells of God's promise to bring the Israelites out from under the burdens of Egypt. With this cup we honor Jewish women throughout history who worked to bring Jews out from under the burdens of poverty, oppression, and anti-semitism in the many Egypts where Jews have lived.

We dedicate this cup to: Doña Gracia Nasi, Emma Lazarus, Hannah Greenebaum Solomon, Bertha Pappenheim, and Rachel Auerbach.

Invite people around the table to add names of women to honor with this cup. Select and read a biography of one of these women from Appendix I. Alternatively, choose a woman from your own family or community and share her story.

Lift your glass for the blessing over the wine/grape juice. Recite the *Kiddush* using one of the following four options; the first two include the full holiday *Kiddush* while the second two include only the brief blessing over the fruit of the vine. After the blessings, drink the first cup.

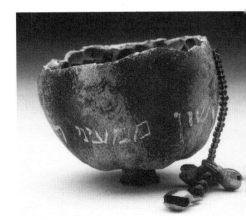

Option 1: Full holiday Kiddush with feminine
God-language. Begin here on Friday night:

(וַיְהִי־עֶרֶב וַיְהִי־בֹקֶר יוֹם הַשִּׁשִּׁי.	(Vay'hi erev vay'hi voker yom hashishi.
וַיְכֻלּוּ הַשָּׁמַיִם וְהָאָרֶץ	Vay'chulu hashamayim v'ha'aretz
וְכָל־צְבָאָם.	v'chol tz'va'am.
וַתְּכַל אֱלֹהִים בַּיּוֹם הַשְּׁבִיעִי	Vat'chal elohim bayom hash'vi'i
מְלַאכְתָּהּ אֲשֶׁר עָשָׂתָה.	m'lachta asher asta.
וַתִּשְׁבֹּת בַּיּוֹם הַשְּׁבִיעִי	Vatishbot bayom hash'vi'i
מִכָּל־מְלַאכְתָּהּ אֲשֶׁר עָשָׂתָה.	mikol m'lachta asher asta.
וַתְּבָרֶךְ אֱלֹהִים אֶת־יוֹם הַשְּׁבִיעִי	Vat'varech elohim et yom hash'vi'i
וַתְּקַדֵּשׁ אֹתוֹ	vat'kadeish oto,
כִּי בוֹ שָׁבְתָה מִכָּל־מְלַאכְתָּהּ	ki vo shavta mikol m'lachta
אֲשֶׁר־בָּרְאָה אֱלֹהִים לַעֲשׂוֹת.)	asher bar'a elohim la'asot.)

Continue here, adding words in parentheses on Shabbat:

בְּרוּכָה אַתְּ יָהּ	B'rucha at yah
אֱלֹהֵינוּ רוּחַ הָעוֹלָם	eloheinu ruach ha'olam
בּוֹרֵאת פְּרִי הַגָּפֶן.	boreit p'ri hagafen.
בְּרוּכָה אַתְּ יָהּ	B'rucha at yah
אֱלֹהֵינוּ רוּחַ הָעוֹלָם	eloheinu ruach ha'olam
אֲשֶׁר בָּחֲרָה־בָנוּ מִכָּל־עָם,	asher bachara vanu mikol am,
וְרוֹמְמַתְנוּ מִכָּל־לָשׁוֹן,	v'rom'matnu mikol lashon,
וְקִדְּשַׁתְנוּ בְּמִצְוֹתֶיהָ.	v'kid'shatnu b'mitzvoteiha.
וַתִּתְּנִי־לָנוּ יָהּ אֱלֹהֵינוּ	Vatit'ni lanu, yah eloheinu,
בְּאַהֲבָה (שַׁבָּתוֹת לִמְנוּחָה וּ)	b'ahava (shabbatot lim'nucha u')
מוֹעֲדִים לְשִׂמְחָה	mo'adim l'simcha,
חַגִּים וּזְמַנִּים לְשָׂשׂוֹן,	chagim uz'manim l'sason,

אֶת יוֹם (הַשַּׁבָּת הַזֶּה וְאֶת יוֹם) | et yom (hashabbat hazeh v'et yom)

חַג הַמַּצּוֹת הַזֶּה | chag hamatzot hazeh,

זְמַן חֵרוּתֵנוּ | z'man cheiruteinu,

(בְּאַהֲבָה) מִקְרָא קֹדֶשׁ | (b'ahava) mikra kodesh,

זֵכֶר לִיצִיאַת מִצְרָיִם. | zeicher litzi'at mitzrayim.

כִּי בָנוּ בָחַרְתָּ וְאוֹתָנוּ קִדַּשְׁתָּ | Ki vanu vachart, v'otanu kidasht,

מִכָּל־הָעַמִּים | mikol ha'amim

(וְשַׁבָּת) וּמוֹעֲדֵי קָדְשֶׁךָ | (v'shabbat) umo'adei kodsheich

(בְּאַהֲבָה וּבְרָצוֹן) | (b'ahava uv'ratzon)

בְּשִׂמְחָה וּבְשָׂשׂוֹן הִנְחַלְתָּנוּ. | b'simcha uv'sason hinchalatnu.

בְּרוּכָה אַתְּ יָהּ מְקַדֶּשֶׁת (הַשַּׁבָּת וְ) | B'rucha at yah m'kadeshet (hashabbat v')

יִשְׂרָאֵל וְהַזְּמַנִּים. | yisraeil v'haz'manim.

On Saturday night, add the following marking the division between Shabbat and the festival:

בְּרוּכָה אַתְּ יָהּ אֱלֹהֵינוּ רוּחַ הָעוֹלָם | Brucha at ya eloheinu ruach ha'olam

בּוֹרֵאת מְאוֹרֵי הָאֵשׁ: | boreit me'orei ha'esh.

בְּרוּכָה אַתְּ יָהּ אֱלֹהֵינוּ רוּחַ הָעוֹלָם | Brucha at yah eloheinu ruach ha'olam

הַמַּבְדִּילָה בֵּין קֹדֶשׁ לְחוֹל | hamavdilah bein kodesh lechol

בֵּין אוֹר לְחֹשֶׁךְ | bein or lechoshech,

בֵּין יִשְׂרָאֵל לָעַמִּים | bein yisrael la'amim

בֵּין יוֹם הַשְּׁבִיעִי לְשֵׁשֶׁת יְמֵי הַמַּעֲשֶׂה: | bein yom hashevi'i lesheshet yemei hama'aseh.

בֵּין קְדֻשַּׁת הַשַּׁבָּת לִקְדֻשַּׁת יוֹם טוֹב | Bein kedushat shabbat likdushat yom tov

הִבְדַּלְתָּ וְאֶת־יוֹם הַשְּׁבִיעִי | hivdalt ve'et yom hashevi'i

מִשֵּׁשֶׁת יְמֵי הַמַּעֲשֶׂה קִדַּשְׁתָּ. | misheshet yemei hama'aseh kidasht.

הִבְדַּלְתָּ וְקִדַּשְׁתָּ אֶת עַמְּךָ יִשְׂרָאֵל בִּקְדֻשָּׁתֶךָ. | Hivdalt vekidasht et ameich yisra'el bikdushatech.

בְּרוּכָה אַתְּ יָהּ הַמַּבְדִּילָה בֵּין קֹדֶשׁ לְחוֹל: | Brucha at yah hamavdilah beyn kodesh lechol.

Option 2: Full holiday Kiddush with traditional language.
Begin here on Friday night:

(וַיְהִי־עֶרֶב וַיְהִי־בֹקֶר יוֹם הַשִּׁשִּׁי.

וַיְכֻלּוּ הַשָּׁמַיִם וְהָאָרֶץ וְכָל־צְבָאָם.

וַיְכַל אֱלֹהִים בַּיּוֹם הַשְּׁבִיעִי

מְלַאכְתּוֹ אֲשֶׁר עָשָׂה.

וַיִּשְׁבֹּת בַּיּוֹם הַשְּׁבִיעִי

מִכָּל־מְלַאכְתּוֹ אֲשֶׁר עָשָׂה.

וַיְבָרֶךְ אֱלֹהִים אֶת־יוֹם הַשְּׁבִיעִי

וַיְקַדֵּשׁ אֹתוֹ

כִּי בוֹ שָׁבַת מִכָּל־מְלַאכְתּוֹ

אֲשֶׁר בָּרָא אֱלֹהִים לַעֲשׂוֹת.)

(Vay'hi erev vay'hi voker yom hashishi.

Vay'chulu hashamayim v'ha'aretz v'chol tz'va'am.

Vay'chal elohim bayom hash'vi'i

m'lachto asher asa.

Vayishbot bayom hash'vi'i

mikol m'lachto asher asa.

Vay'varech elohim et yom hash'vi'i

vay'kadeish oto,

ki vo shavat mikol m'lachto

asher bara elohim la'asot.)

Continue here adding words in parentheses on Shabbat:

בָּרוּךְ אַתָּה יְיָ

אֱלֹהֵינוּ מֶלֶךְ הָעוֹלָם

בּוֹרֵא פְּרִי הַגָּפֶן.

בָּרוּךְ אַתָּה יְיָ

אֱלֹהֵינוּ מֶלֶךְ הָעוֹלָם

אֲשֶׁר בָּחַר־בָּנוּ מִכָּל־עָם

וְרוֹמְמָנוּ מִכָּל־לָשׁוֹן

וְקִדְּשָׁנוּ בְּמִצְוֹתָיו.

וַתִּתֶּן־לָנוּ יְיָ אֱלֹהֵינוּ

בְּאַהֲבָה (שַׁבָּתוֹת לִמְנוּחָה וּ)

מוֹעֲדִים לְשִׂמְחָה

Baruch atah adonai

eloheinu melech ha'olam

borei p'ri hagafen.

Baruch atah adonai

eloheinu melech ha'olam

asher bachar banu mikol am,

v'rom'manu mikol lashon,

v'kid'shanu b'mitzvotav.

Vatiten lanu, adonai eloheinu,

b'ahava (shabatot limnucha u')

mo'adim l'simcha,

חַגִּים וּזְמַנִּים לְשָׂשׂוֹן	chagim uz'manim l'sason,
אֶת יוֹם (הַשַּׁבָּת הַזֶּה וְאֶת יוֹם)	et yom (hashabat hazeh v'et yom)
חַג הַמַּצּוֹת הַזֶּה זְמַן חֵרוּתֵנוּ	chag hamatzot hazeh, z'man cheiruteinu,
(בְּאַהֲבָה) מִקְרָא קֹדֶשׁ	(b'ahava) mikra kodesh,
זֵכֶר לִיצִיאַת מִצְרָיִם.	zeicher litzi'at mitzrayim.
כִּי בָנוּ בָחַרְתָּ וְאוֹתָנוּ קִדַּשְׁתָּ	Ki vanu vacharta, v'otanu kidashta,
מִכָּל־הָעַמִּים	mikol ha'amim
(וְשַׁבָּת) וּמוֹעֲדֵי קָדְשְׁךָ	(v'shabbat) umo'adei kodsh'cha
(בְּאַהֲבָה וּבְרָצוֹן)	(b'ahava uv'ratzon)
בְּשִׂמְחָה וּבְשָׂשׂוֹן הִנְחַלְתָּנוּ.	b'simcha uv'sason hinchaltanu.
בָּרוּךְ אַתָּה יְיָ	Baruch atah adonai
מְקַדֵּשׁ (הַשַּׁבָּת וְ)	m'kadeish (hashabbat v')
יִשְׂרָאֵל וְהַזְּמַנִּים.	yisraeil v'haz'manim.

On Saturday night, add the following, marking the division between Shabbat and the festival:

בָּרוּךְ אַתָּה יְיָ אֱלֹהֵינוּ מֶלֶךְ הָעוֹלָם	Baruch ata adonai eloheinu melech ha'olam
בּוֹרֵא מְאוֹרֵי הָאֵשׁ:	borei me'orei ha'esh.
בָּרוּךְ אַתָּה יְיָ אֱלֹהֵינוּ מֶלֶךְ הָעוֹלָם	Baruch ata adonai eloheinu melech ha'olam
הַמַּבְדִּיל בֵּין קֹדֶשׁ לְחוֹל	hamavdil bein kodesh lechol
בֵּין אוֹר לְחֹשֶׁךְ בֵּין יִשְׂרָאֵל לָעַמִּים	bein or lechoshech, bein yisrael la'amim
בֵּין יוֹם הַשְּׁבִיעִי לְשֵׁשֶׁת יְמֵי הַמַּעֲשֶׂה:	bein yom hashevi'i lesheshet yemei hama'aseh.
בֵּין קְדֻשַּׁת הַשַּׁבָּת לִקְדֻשַּׁת	Bein kedushat shabbat likdushat
יוֹם טוֹב הִבְדַּלְתָּ וְאֶת־יוֹם הַשְּׁבִיעִי	yom tov hivdalta ve'et yom hashevi'i
מִשֵּׁשֶׁת יְמֵי הַמַּעֲשֶׂה קִדַּשְׁתָּ.	misheshet yemei hama'aseh kidashta.
הִבְדַּלְתָּ וְקִדַּשְׁתָּ אֶת עַמְּךָ	Hivdalta vekidashta et am'cha
יִשְׂרָאֵל בִּקְדֻשָּׁתֶךָ.	yisra'el bikdushatecha.
בָּרוּךְ אַתָּה יְיָ הַמַּבְדִּיל	Baruch ata adonai hamavdil
בֵּין קֹדֶשׁ לְחוֹל:	beyn kodesh lechol.

כוס ראשון KOS RISHON THE FIRST CUP 40

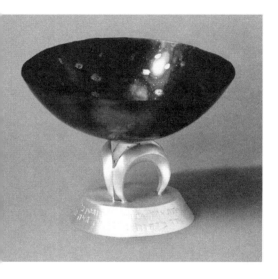

(And it was evening and it was morning, the sixth day. Heaven, earth, and all hosts were finished. On the seventh day, God completed the work that had been done, and ceased upon the seventh day from all the work that had been done. God blessed the seventh day and made it holy. For on it God rested from all the work of creation that God had done.)

You are Blessed, Our God, Spirit of the World, who creates the fruit of the vine. You are Blessed, Our God, Spirit of the World, who has chosen us and distinguished us by sanctifying us with the *mitzvot*. You have lovingly favored us with (Shabbat for rest and) festivals for joy, seasons and holidays for happiness, among them (this Shabbat and) this day of *Pesach*, the season of our liberation, a day of sacred assembly commemorating the Exodus from Egypt. You have chosen us, sanctifying us among all peoples by granting us (Shabbat and) Your sacred festivals (lovingly and gladly) in joy and happiness. You are Blessed, Our God, who sanctifies (Shabbat and) the people of Israel and the festival seasons.

(You are Blessed, Our God, Spirit of the World, who creates the light of the fire. You are Blessed, Our God, Spirit of the World, who separates between holy and ordinary, light and dark, the seventh day and the six days of work. You separate between the holiness of Shabbat and the holiness of a festival. You set apart the seventh day from the six days of the week. You separate and sanctify your people Israel with your holiness. You are Blessed, Our God, Spirit of the World, who separates the holy from the ordinary.)

Option 3: Short blessing for wine or grape juice
with feminine God-language

בְּרוּכָה אַתְּ יָהּ
אֱלֹהֵינוּ רוּחַ הָעוֹלָם
בּוֹרֵאת פְּרִי הַגָּפֶן.

B'rucha at yah
eloheinu ruach ha'olam
boreit p'ri hagafen.

You are Blessed, Our God, Spirit of the World,
who creates the fruit of the vine.

Option 4: Short blessing for wine or grape juice
with traditional God-language

בָּרוּךְ אַתָּה יְיָ
אֱלֹהֵינוּ מֶלֶךְ הָעוֹלָם
בּוֹרֵא פְּרִי הַגָּפֶן.

Baruch atah adonai
eloheinu melech ha'olam
borei p'ri hagafen.

You are Blessed, Our God, Spirit of the World,
who creates the fruit of the vine.

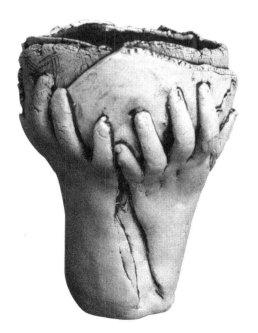

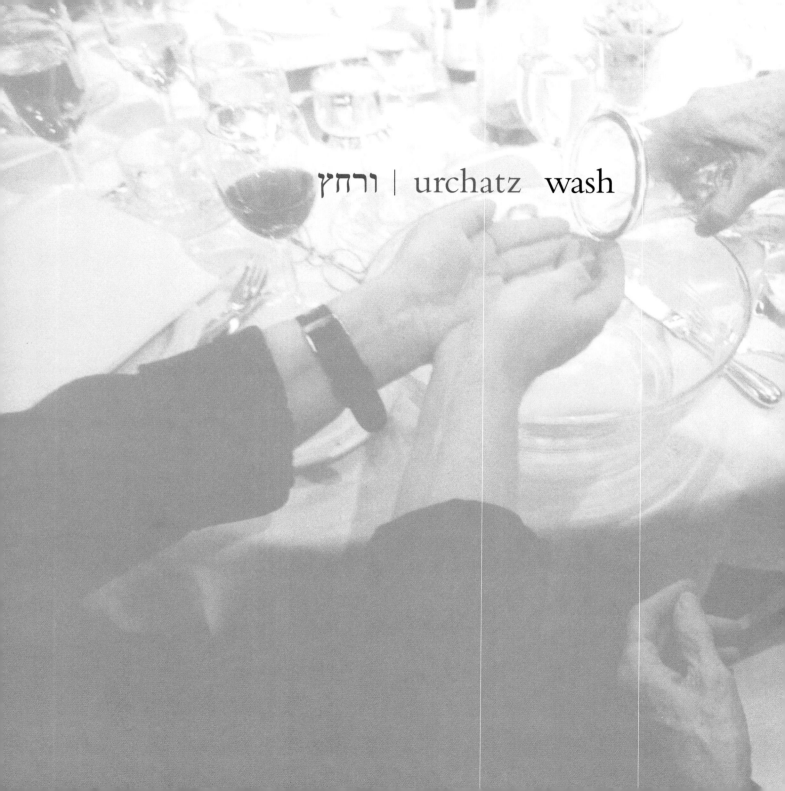

ורחץ | urchatz wash

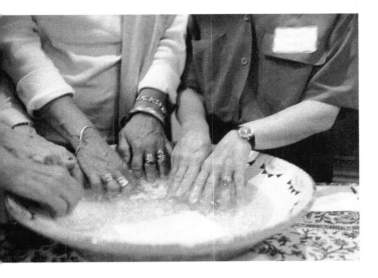

From wine, we step back to water. This time not the water of Miriam's Well, but the waters of the ancient Nile.

The daughter of Pharoah immerses herself.

Deep beneath the gentle current she hears a faint persistent cry.

She emerges from the water and wipes the droplets from her eyelashes.

It is then that she spots the basket. She is not the only one in the water seeking renewal.

Fear and context fade away. The daughter of Pharoah reaches out to Moshe and cradles him in her arms.

ALL

May the water we offer each other now, bring us closer to their embrace.

If everyone is participating in this hand-washing, pass around a bowl of water and a pitcher or washing cup. Each person can wash the hands of the person sitting to her right. Otherwise, one person can be chosen to carry out this symbolic washing on behalf of the entire group. No blessing is recited.

כרפס | karpas   fruit of the earth

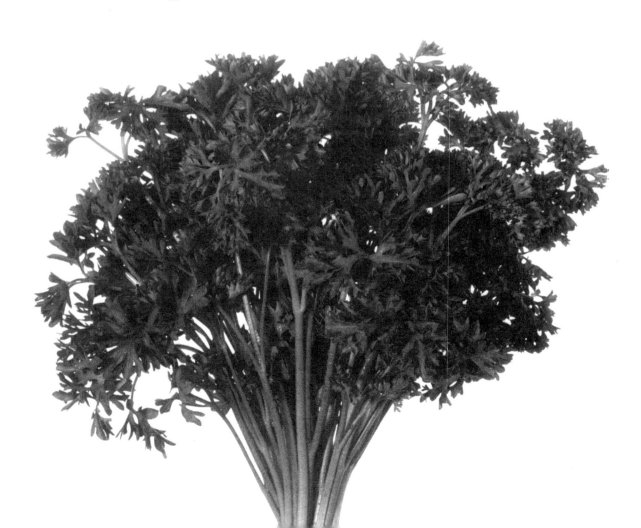

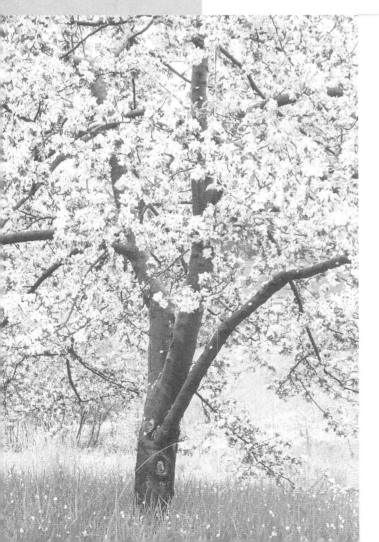

COMMENTARY

Seder tables throughout the ages have featured different vegetables for *karpas*, depending on availability. While most people use parsley, some use celery or potatoes. Others offer a variety of vegetables and dips. *Karpas* probably began as an adaptation of the appetizers served at Greek and Roman banquets. As one of the names for Passover is *Chag Ha'aviv*, the Festival of Spring, *karpas* has also come to symbolize spring. The Song of Songs, which uses images of spring in the natural world to celebrate sexuality and love, is traditionally read during the Shabbat of Passover, but some sing portions of it during the *karpas* ritual.

READERS

Long before the struggle upward begins,
there is tremor in the seed.
Self-protection cracks,
Roots reach down and grab hold.
The seed swells, and tender shoots
push up toward light.
This is *karpas*: spring awakening growth.
A force so tough it can break stone.

And why do we dip *karpas* into salt water?

To remember the sweat and tears of our ancestors in bondage.

To taste the bitter tears of our earth, unable to fully renew itself this spring because of our waste, neglect, and greed.

To feel the sting of society's refusal to celebrate the blossoming of women's bodies and the full range of our capacity for love.

And why should salt water be touched by *karpas*?

ALL

To remind us that tears stop. Spring comes. And with it the potential for change.

Dip the *karpas* into the salt water. Say the blessing and eat the *karpas* while reclining as a sign of freedom.

בְּרוּכָה אַתְּ יָהּ אֱלֹהֵינוּ רוּחַ הָעוֹלָם
בּוֹרֵאת פְּרִי הָאֲדָמָה.

B'rucha at yah eloheinu ruach ha'olam
boreit p'ri ha'adama.

or

בָּרוּךְ אַתָּה יְיָ אֱלֹהֵינוּ מֶלֶךְ הָעוֹלָם
בּוֹרֵא פְּרִי הָאֲדָמָה.

Baruch atah adonai eloheinu melech ha'olam
borei p'ri ha'adama.

You are Blessed, Our God, Spirit of the World, who creates the fruit of the earth.

Do Something! The symbolism of *karpas* raises many issues that call for action. To find out how to fight unfair labor practices and the continued existence of sweatshops, call Jews for Racial and Economic Justice. Join a local environmental action group or start a Jewish environmental group in your area by calling the Coalition on the Environment and Jewish Life. Bring a speaker to discuss issues concerning Jewish women and girls, body image, and eating disorders to your community or to your child's school by contacting Ma'yan about their girls' initiative, Koach Banot. (For more information and web addresses for these organizations, see Appendix III.)

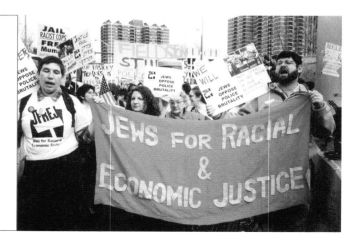

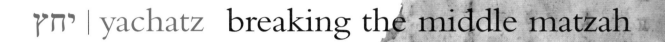

יחץ | yachatz   breaking the middle matzah

Break the middle of the three *matzot* on the seder table and
wrap the larger broken piece in a napkin. Set aside this
broken piece of matzah, called the *afikoman*. The following
meditation offers one possible meaning for the symbolic act
of breaking the matzah. It is followed by the *Mi Shebeirach*,
a prayer for healing.

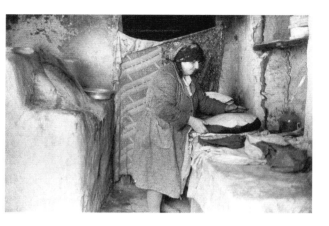

Some do not get the chance to rise and spread out like golden loaves of challah, filled with sweet raisins and crowned with shiny braids.

Rushed, neglected, not kneaded by caring hands, we grow up afraid that any touch might cause a break. There are some ingredients we never receive.

Tonight, let us bless our cracked surfaces and sharp edges, unafraid to see our brittleness and brave enough to see our beauty.

Reaching for wholeness, let us piece together the parts of ourselves we have found and honor all that is still hidden.

מי שברך | MI SHEBEIRACH

מִי שֶׁבֵּרַךְ אֲבוֹתֵינוּ
מְקוֹר הַבְּרָכָה לְאִמּוֹתֵינוּ

Mi shebeirach avoteinu
M'kor habracha l'imoteinu

May the source of strength who blessed
the ones before us,
Help us find the courage to make our lives a blessing
And let us say: Amen.

מִי שֶׁבֵּרַךְ אִמּוֹתֵינוּ
מְקוֹר הַבְּרָכָה לְאֲבוֹתֵינוּ

Mi shebeirach imoteinu
M'kor habracha l'avoteinu

Bless those in need of healing with refuah sh'leimah,
The renewal of body, the renewal of spirit
And let us say: Amen.

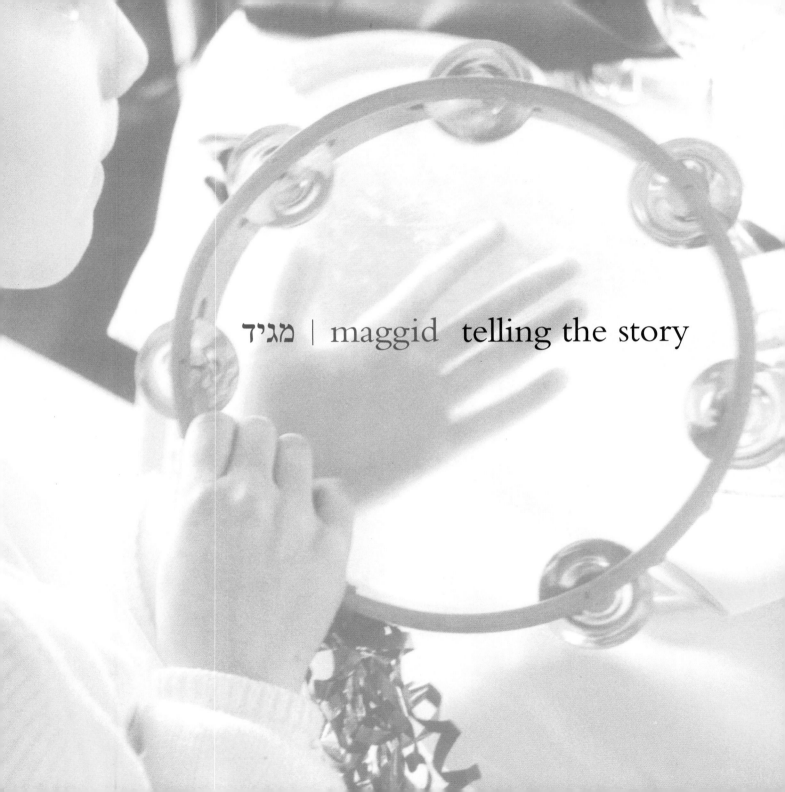

מגיד | maggid telling the story

The *maggid* is the heart of the Haggadah. The word *maggid* comes from the same Hebrew root as the word Haggadah. The root means to tell. This section of the Haggadah contains the story of the Exodus. The story is not a neat narrative with a beginning, middle, and end. A pastiche of questions, rituals, biblical passages, and tales from different moments in Jewish history, the *maggid's* structure invites us to use our own creativity in retelling and re-experiencing the Exodus.

Turn down the covering of the *matzot* to reveal the broken matzah. Raise the seder plate or pass it around to arouse interest in all the symbols that will be discussed during the *maggid*. Sing the traditional *Ha Lachma Anya* text in Aramaic.

הא לחמא

HA LACHMA

הָא לַחְמָא

Ha lachma

הָא לַחְמָא עַנְיָא

Ha lachma anya

דִּי־אֲכָלוּ

di achalu

דִּי־אֲכָלוּ אֲבָהָתָנָא/אִמְהָתָנָא

di achalu avahatana/imhatana

בְּאַרְעָא בְּאַרְעָא דְמִצְרָיִם.

b'ara, b'ara d'mitzrayim.

כָּל־דִכְפִין יֵיתֵי וְיֵכוֹל.

Kol dichfin yeitei v'yeichol.

כָּל־דִצְרִיךְ יֵיתֵי וְיִפְסַח.

Kol ditzrich yeitei v'yifsach.

הָשַׁתָּא הָכָא.

Hashata hacha.

לְשָׁנָה הַבָּאָה בְּאַרְעָא דְיִשְׂרָאֵל.

L'shana haba'a b'ara d'yisraeil.

הָשַׁתָּא עַבְדֵי.

Hashata avdei.

לְשָׁנָה הַבָּאָה בְּנֵי וּבְנוֹת חוֹרִין:

L'shana haba'a b'nei uv'not chorin.

This is the bread of affliction our ancestors ate in the land of Egypt. Let all who are hungry come and eat. Let all who are in need come and share our Passover. This year we are here. Next year in the Land of Israel. This year we are slaves. Next year, may we all be free.

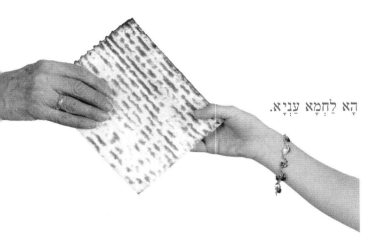

הָא לַחְמָא עַנְיָא.

Ha lachma anya.
This bread, the symbol of freedom, is also the bread of affliction.

We eat this bread of poverty and hardship even as we celebrate our freedom because, as Jews, we must build sanctuaries with windows and doors that open to the world.

הָא לַחְמָא עַנְיָא.

Ha lachma anya.
Hunger continues to plague an estimated 840 million people around the world; 30 million in the United States.

דִי־אֲכָלוּ אִמְהָתָנָא.

Di achalu imhatana.
Seventy percent of the world's poor are female. The United States has the highest child poverty rate of any industrialized nation: one in every five American children is poor.

כָּל־דִכְפִין יֵיתֵי וְיֵכוֹל.

Kol dichfin yeitei v'yeichol.
When will all who are hungry come and eat?

When we feel their hunger as our own. When we take responsibility for the injustice that surrounds us by committing to *tikkun olam* and *tzedakah*— healing the world, doing justice, and sharing our resources.

ALL

הָשַׁתָּא עַבְדֵי.

Hashata avdei.
Until hunger is eliminated we remain slaves. Only when all are nourished will we be free.

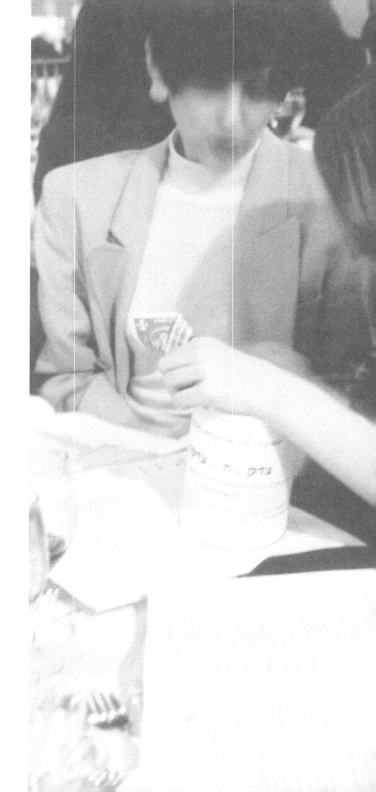

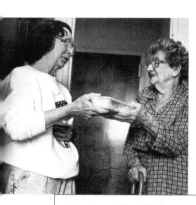

Do Something! Collect *tzedakah* or *tzedakah* pledges. Bring food to a local shelter. Buy lunch for a homeless person. Approximate how much money you would spend to invite one extra guest to your seder, and donate that money to Mazon: A Jewish Response to Hunger. Support the Jewish FundS for Justice Women's Poverty Purim Fund and TZEDEC community investment program. Support the New Israel Fund's Economic Empowerment for Women, dedicated to improving the lives of low-income women and their families through economic empowerment. Contribute to YEDID's program for low-income, often single-parent, Israeli women that stresses financial literacy skills as well as direct assistance.

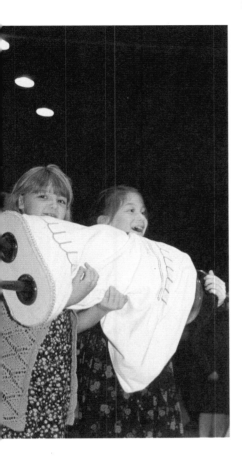

Fill your second cup and cover the three ceremonial *matzot*.
According to tradition, the youngest child leads the singing
of the Four Questions in any language. All youngest children,
regardless of age, can join.

READERS

I learned the Four Questions in the kitchen.
My mother handed me a towel and said: "I'll wash,
you dry. I'll sing a few words, and you repeat."
And so we sang, from the night after Purim, every
night until I'd learned it all.

I taught the Four Questions at bath time to two
little ones, lithe and slippery as seals. "I'll sing a
few words, and then you sing," I said. They
loved to dip and splash for "*sh'tei f'amim*." And
so we sang, from Purim to Pesach. Every night,
until they learned it all.

This is a rite of passage. We learn our part
and take our turn.

Wine trembles in our cups. Candles flicker.
Conversation stops.

First we ask the prescribed questions.
Then, we add our own.

מַה־נִּשְׁתַּנָּה הַלַּיְלָה הַזֶּה
מִכָּל־הַלֵּילוֹת?
שֶׁבְּכָל־הַלֵּילוֹת אָנוּ אוֹכְלִין
חָמֵץ וּמַצָּה
הַלַּיְלָה הַזֶּה כֻּלּוֹ מַצָּה:
שֶׁבְּכָל־הַלֵּילוֹת אָנוּ אוֹכְלִין
שְׁאָר יְרָקוֹת
הַלַּיְלָה הַזֶּה מָרוֹר:
שֶׁבְּכָל־הַלֵּילוֹת אֵין אָנוּ מַטְבִּילִין
אֲפִילוּ פַּעַם אֶחָת
הַלַּיְלָה הַזֶּה שְׁתֵּי פְעָמִים:
שֶׁבְּכָל־הַלֵּילוֹת אָנוּ אוֹכְלִין
בֵּין יוֹשְׁבִין וּבֵין מְסֻבִּין
הַלַּיְלָה הַזֶּה כֻּלָּנוּ מְסֻבִּין:

Ma nishtana halaila hazeh

mikol haleilot? (2x)

Sheb'chol haleilot anu ochlin

chameitz umatzah (2x)

Halaila hazeh (2x) *kulo matzah.* (2x)

Sheb'chol haleilot anu ochlin

sh'ar y'rakot (2x)

Halaila hazeh (2x) *maror.* (2x)

Sheb'chol haleilot ein anu matbilin

afilu pa'am echat (2x)

halaila hazeh (2x) *sh'tei f'amim.* (2x)

Sheb'chol haleilot anu ochlin

bein yoshvin uvein m'subin (2x)

halaila hazeh (2x) *kulanu m'subin.* (2x)

How different is this night from all other nights! On all other nights we eat *chameitz* and matzah, why on this night do we eat only matzah? On all other nights we eat other kinds of vegetables, why on this night do we eat only *maror*? On all other nights we do not dip even once, why on this night do we dip twice? On all other nights we eat either sitting or reclining, why on this night do we all recline?

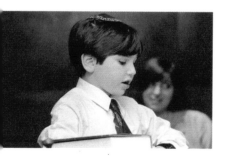

Share additional questions about the seder, the Haggadah, and the meaning of freedom and slavery. Use the rest of the seder to answer and discuss these questions.

COMMENTARY

To answer the question of why this night is different we begin the first telling of the story of slavery and redemption. Here the traditional text alternates with the imagined voices of Shifra and Puah, the Hebrew midwives whose heroism opens the Exodus story.

READERS

עֲבָדִים הָיִינוּ לְפַרְעֹה בְּמִצְרָיִם.

Avadim hayinu l'pharoh b'mitzrayim.

We were slaves to Pharaoh in Egypt.

שְׁפָחוֹת הָיִינוּ לְפַרְעֹה בְּמִצְרָיִם.

Sh'fachot hayinu l'pharoh b'mitzrayim.

We, Shifra and Puah, were slaves to Pharaoh in Egypt. We were also midwives and respected leaders in our community. When Pharoah decreed that we put all baby boys to death, we were not able to comply. For we felt the mighty hand of God in our outstretched arms as we helped bring Israelite infants into the world.

וַתּוֹצִיאֵנוּ יָהּ מִשָּׁם

Vatotzi'einu yah misham

בְּיָד חֲזָקָה וּבִזְרוֹעַ נְטוּיָה.

b'yad chazaka uvizro'a n'tuya.

וְאִלּוּ לֹא הוֹצִיאָה מְקוֹר חַיֵּינוּ

V'ilu lo hotzi'a m'kor chayeinu

אֶת־אֲבוֹתֵינוּ וְאֶת־אִמּוֹתֵינוּ מִמִּצְרַיִם

et avoteinu v'et imoteinu mimitzrayim,

הֲרֵי אָנוּ וְצֶאֱצָאֵינוּ

harei anu v'tze'etza'einu,

וְצֶאֱצָאֵי עַמֵּנוּ

v'tze'etza'ei ameinu

מְשֻׁעְבָּדִים הָיִינוּ

m'shubadim hayinu

לְפַרְעֹה בְּמִצְרָיִם.

l'pharoh b'mitzrayim.

56

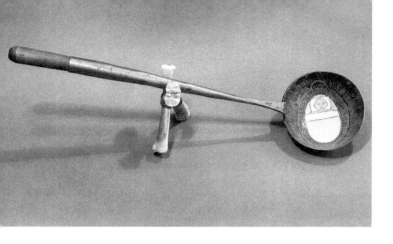

And God brought us out of Egypt with a mighty hand and an outstretched arm. But if the Source of Life had not brought our ancestors out of Egypt,

And if we, Shifra and Puah, and Yocheved and Miriam and the daughter of Pharoah, and Moses and Aaron had not taken the risks we took, we and our children and our children's children would still be enslaved to Pharaoh in Egypt.

וַאֲפִלוּ כֻּלָנוּ חֲכָמִים
כֻּלָנוּ נְבוֹנִים כֻּלָנוּ זְקֵנִים
כֻּלָנוּ יוֹדְעִים אֶת־הַתּוֹרָה
מִצְוָה עָלֵינוּ לְסַפֵּר בִּיצִיאַת מִצְרָיִם.

Va'afilu kulanu chachamim,

kulanu n'vonim, kulanu z'keinim,

kulanu yod'im et hatorah,

mitzva aleinu l'sapeir bitzi'at mitzrayim.

So even if all of us were wise, all of us understanding, all of us old, all of us learned in the Torah, it would still be incumbent upon us to tell the story of the Exodus from Egypt.

וְכָל הַמַּרְבֶּה לְסַפֵּר בִּיצִיאַת מִצְרַיִם
הֲרֵי זֶה מְשֻׁבָּח.

V'chol hamarbeh l'sapeir bitzi'at mitzrayim

harei zeh m'shubach.

And all who elaborate the story of the Exodus deserve praise. And the telling that includes the actions of women is exalted.

עבדים היינו

AVADIM HAYINU

עֲבָדִים הָיִינוּ הָיִינוּ
עַתָּה בְּנֵי חוֹרִין וּבְנוֹת חוֹרִין.
עֲבָדִים הָיִינוּ
עַתָּה עַתָּה בְּנֵי חוֹרִין.
עֲבָדִים הָיִינוּ
עַתָּה עַתָּה בְּנוֹת חוֹרִין בְּנוֹת חוֹרִין.

Avadim hayinu, hayinu.
Ata b'nei chorin u'vnot chorin.
Avadim hayinu
Ata, ata b'nei chorin.
Avadim hayinu
Ata, Ata b'not chorin, b'not chorin. (2x)

We were slaves, now we are free.

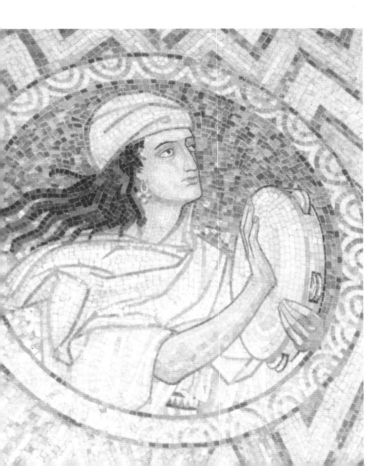

READERS

In a traditional seder, we tell the story of sages in the second century who gathered in B'nei B'rak to discuss the Exodus from Egypt. All were activists in the struggle against Rome. They talked through the night until their students, standing watch, alerted them with the words: *raboteinu, higi'a z'man...* The time has come to recite the morning *Sh'ma*. Tonight we remember the subversive courage of teachers of our own generation.

On the 22nd of Kislev 5749 (December 1, 1988), an extraordinary group of women from the United States and Israel, Canada and Great Britain, Brazil and West Germany, Argentina and South Africa, New Zealand and Sweden, 70 women strong, carried a *Sefer Torah* to the *Kotel*.

And they were so intent on praying together, Conservative women with Reform, Orthodox with Reconstructionist, so engrossed in the blending of separate voices and traditions, so at one with that sweet and holy sound, that they ignored the curses from beyond the *m'chitzah*.

They formed a circle around the Torah and read from it aloud until the clear, bright syllables bounced against the ancient stones, shattered, recombined, and echoed back across the Plaza, across Jerusalem.

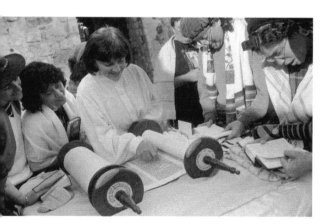

ALL

רַבּוֹתֵינוּ מוֹרוֹתֵנוּ	Raboteinu, moroteinu, our rabbis and teachers.
הִגִּיעַ זְמַן	higi'a z'man, it is time.
רַבּוֹתֵינוּ אֲחִיוֹתֵנוּ	raboteinu, achyoteinu. Our rabbis and sisters,
הִגִּיעַ זְמַן	higi'a z'man....

KADDISH D'RABBANAN
קדיש דרבנן

For our teachers and their students
And the students of the students.
We ask for peace and loving kindness
and let us say: Amen.
And for those who study Torah,
here and everywhere,
May they be blessed with all they need.
And let us say: Amen.
We ask for peace and loving kindness
And let us say: Amen. (2x)

Do Something! Support Advancing Women Professionals
(AWP) as they promote the leadership of women
professionals within Jewish institutions at the national and
local levels. Give a subscription of *Lilith* Magazine or
*Nashim: A Journal of Jewish Women's Studies & Gender
Issues* or *HEEB: The New Jewish Review* to your local
library, Hillel, high school or religious school. Learn how or
volunteer to read Torah or lead services in your community.

ארבעה בנות ARBA'A BANOT THE FOUR DAUGHTERS

COMMENTARY

The traditional text of the four children consists of a dialogue between four different sons and their father. The dialogue emphasizes the need to approach different learners with different approaches, but it ignores the possibility of female students and teachers. Many contemporary *Haggadot* rectify this absence by changing "sons" to "children" and "father" to "parent." The following reading uses the structure of the original text to imagine four different responses to a seder that puts women's issues in the forefront.

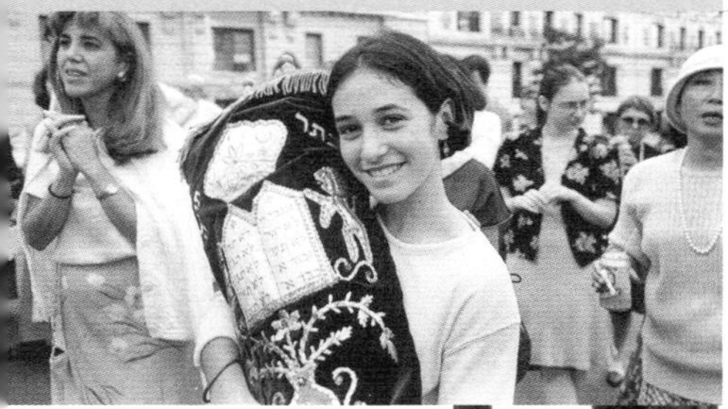

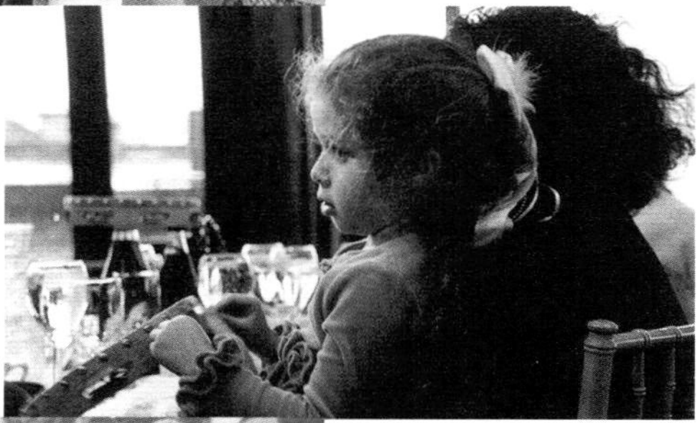

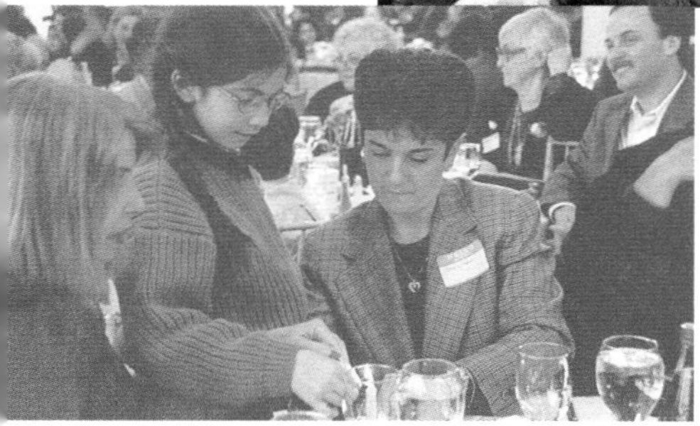

READERS

The daughter in search of a usable past. *Ma hi omeret?* What does she say?

"Why didn't the Torah count women among the '600,000 men on foot, aside from children,' who came out of Egypt? And why did Moses say at Sinai, 'Go not near a woman,' addressing only men, as if preparation for Revelation was not meant for us, as well?"

Because she already understands that Jewish memory is essential to our identity, teach her that history is made by those who tell the tale. If Torah did not name and number women, it is up to her to fill the empty spaces of our holy texts.

And the daughter who wants to erase her difference. *Ma hi omeret?* What does she say?

"Why must you keep pushing your women's questions into every text? And why are these women's issues so important to you?"

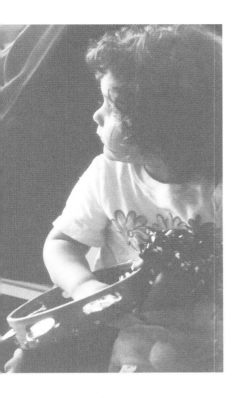

"To you," and "not to me." Since she so easily forgets the struggles of her mothers and sisters, you must tell her the story of your own journey to the seder table and invite her to join you in thanking God for the blessing of being a Jewish woman.

And the daughter who does not know that she has a place at the table. *Ma hi omeret?* What does she say?

"What is this?"

Because she doesn't realize that her question is, in itself, a part of the seder tradition, teach her that the Haggadah is an extended conversation about liberation, and tell her that her insights and questions are also text.

And the daughter who asks no questions?

You must say to her, "Your questions, when they come, will liberate you from Egypt. This is how it is and has always been with your mothers and grandmothers. From the moment Yocheved, Miriam and the midwives questioned Pharaoh's edict until today, every question we ask helps us leave Egypt farther behind."

L'CHI LACH לכי לך

לְכִי לָךְ
L'chi lach,
to a land that I will show you

לֵךְ לְךָ
Leich l'cha,
to a place you do not know

לְכִי לָךְ
L'chi lach,
on your journey I will bless you
And you shall be a blessing (3x)

לְכִי לָךְ
L'chi lach.

לְכִי לָךְ
L'chi lach,
and I shall make your name great

לֵךְ לְךָ
Leich l'cha,
and all shall praise your name

לְכִי לָךְ
L'chi lach,
to the place that I will show you

לְשִׂמְחַת חַיִּים
L'simchat chayim (3x)

לְכִי לָךְ
L'chi lach.

And you shall be a blessing (3x)

לְכִי לָךְ
L'chi lach.

Do Something! Help young people begin to ask their own questions. Support the intern programs at the Jewish Organizing Initiative and AVODAH: The Jewish Service Corps. Find out how you can start a girl's Rosh Hodesh group to empower adolescent girls in your community by contacting Moving Traditions.

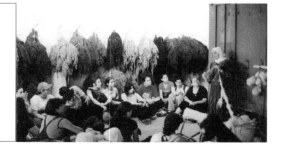

COMMENTARY

This next answer to the original question of how this night is different
goes back to the time before Egyptian slavery to tell the story of how the
Israelites found themselves in Egypt. While the traditional Haggadah focuses
exclusively on the lives of the Patriarchs, this poem offers a vision of the
lives of the Matriarchs and their journey to and eventually out of Egypt.

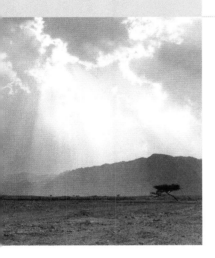

READERS

At first our mothers were like willows, bowing
earthward to the soil. And then, they left their
parents' homes, loved wandering men, and
followed them under huge skies, charged with
stars and the slow progress of barren moons.

Our mothers measured time from month to month.
And when they conceived, carried, bore, nursed,
weaned, struggled for, fought for, lost and wept for
their children, the stars answered with a laugh
and the wind with a promise.

And the slow moon followed their children and
children's children down to Egypt, where they
sojourned and were later enslaved and forced to
bow earthward, to the soil.

Until, after 400 years, the promise was kept
and God drew them out of their narrow
confinement, and brought them out of Egypt
to follow the Covenant under huge skies,
charged with stars.

וְהִיא שֶׁעָמְדָה V'HI SHE'AMDA   IT IS SHE WHO SUSTAINED

COMMENTARY

In a traditional Haggadah, the *V'hi She'amda* emphasizes the fact that the Egyptians were not the only ones in Jewish history who oppressed the Jewish people. According to a commentary by Rabbi Tzvi Hirsh Kalischer (1795-1874), the first word of the Hebrew, וְהִיא V'hi, "And She" (which literally refers to the promise of the covenant which has stood the test of time), can be read as a reference to the *Sh'chinah*, the feminine aspect of God.

Cover the *matzot*, raise a cup of wine or grape juice and recite the following.

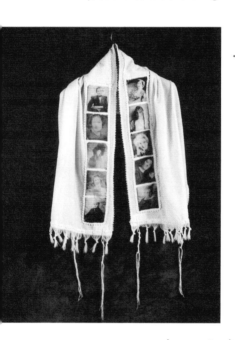

וְהִיא שֶׁעָמְדָה
לַאֲבוֹתֵינוּ וּלְאִמּוֹתֵינוּ וְלָנוּ.
שֶׁלֹּא אֶחָד בִּלְבָד
עָמַד עָלֵינוּ לְכַלּוֹתֵנוּ
אֶלָּא שֶׁבְּכָל דּוֹר וָדוֹר
עוֹמְדִים עָלֵינוּ לְכַלּוֹתֵנוּ
וְהַקָּדוֹשָׁה בְּרוּכָה הִיא
מַצִּילֵנוּ מִיָּדָם:

V'hi she'amda
la'avoteinu ul'imoteinu velanu.
Shelo echad bil'vad
amad aleinu l'chaloteinu
ela sheb'chol dor vador
om'dim aleinu l'chaloteinu
v'hak'dusha b'rucha hi
matzileinu miyadam.

It is She who sustained our ancestors and us.
For not just one has risen to destroy us. In every generation there are those who seek our destruction. But the Holy Blessed One saves us from their hands.

READERS

וְהִיא שֶׁעָמְדָה לַאֲבוֹתֵינוּ וּלְאִמּוֹתֵינוּ וְלָנוּ.   V'hi she'am'da la'avoteinu ul'imoteinu velanu

It is She, the *Sh'chinah*, who sustained our ancestors and us.

65

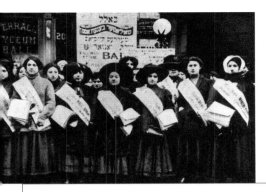

Do something! Contribute a book about Jewish women's history to your local library or synagogue. Encourage your synagogue or school to use the Jewish Women's Archive's curriculum, *Making our Wilderness Bloom: Women who Made American Jewish History,* and help promote Women's History Month. Record your own personal history.

It is She who has dwelt within the hearts and souls of those who have resisted their oppression in every generation.

She dwelled among the judges, prophets, queens, and warriors who in our early history led our people and protected them against those seeking their destruction.

She inspired the Conversos to preserve their faith during the Spanish Inquisition.

She fueled the dreams of early Zionist pioneers who envisioned a new and equal society in an ancient land.

She energized the Bundist organizers who called Her Justice and Revolution.

She strengthened the American immigrant women who organized kosher meat boycotts, labor unions, settlement houses, and aid societies.

She gave courage to the ghetto fighters and kindergarten teachers, the partisans and the rape survivors, the recipe recorders and the food smugglers and all who struggled against evil during the Holocaust.

It is She, the *Sh'chinah* who dwells among all seekers of freedom and justice, and sustains us.

Set down the cup and uncover the *matzot* for the continuation of the telling.

COMMENTARY

In a traditional Haggadah, this section consists of an interplay between verses in Deuteronomy and rabbinic commentary on those verses. The following new commentary on one of the verses invites an examination of the cyclical nature of oppression.

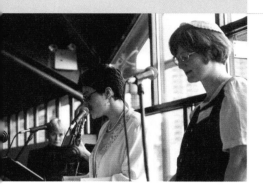

READERS

Go forth and learn. All who have been oppressed can also oppress.

Sarah our Mother oppressed her Egyptian maidservant Hagar. Sarah was barren and she wanted a child. She gave Hagar, her Egyptian maidservant, to Abraham as a wife. When Hagar conceived and became pregnant Sarah grew lesser in her eyes. So Sarah oppressed her and Hagar ran away, as it says:

וַתְּעַנֶּהָ שָׂרַי וַתִּבְרַח מִפָּנֶיהָ:

"V'ta'aneiha Sarai v'tivrach mipaneyha" (GENESIS 16:6).

Go forth and learn: Pharaoh the Egyptian oppressed our people when they dwelled in Egypt.

The Israelites descended to Egypt and lived there. When then they became a nation—great, mighty and numerous—Pharaoh feared that the Egyptians would be overcome by the great multitudes of Israelites, so he decreed that every male child born to an Israelite woman be thrown into the Nile. And the Egyptians treated us harshly and oppressed us; they imposed hard labor on us, as it says:

וַיָּרֵעוּ אֹתָנוּ הַמִּצְרִים וַיְעַנּוּנוּ וַיִּתְּנוּ
עָלֵינוּ עֲבֹדָה קָשָׁה:

"Vayarei'u otanu hamitzrim va'y'anunu va'yitnu aleinu avoda kasha" (DEUTERONOMY 26:6).

This you should never forget: the same word used for Hagar's oppression at the hands of Sarah is used for the Israelites' oppression at the hands of the Egyptians.

This too you should never forget: The children of Israel were saved through the brave and righteous acts of two women: one Hebrew and one Egyptian. Miriam and the daughter of Pharoah.

Go forth and learn: It is easier to oppress than to be free. "Until all of us are free none of us is free" (EMMA LAZARUS, *EPISTLE TO THE HEBREWS*).

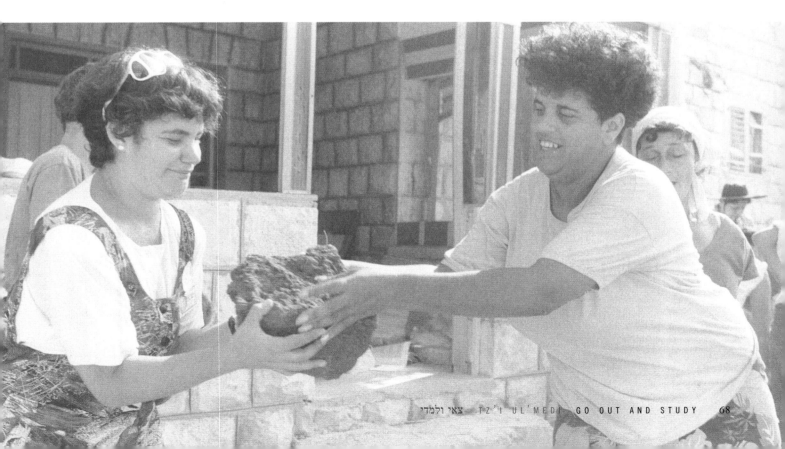

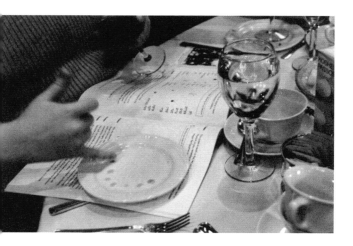

Chant in Hebrew and/or English, removing one drop
of wine or grape juice from your cup for each plague.

READERS

We are about to recite the Ten Plagues. As we call
out the words, we remove ten drops from our
overflowing cups, not by tilting the cup and
spilling some out, but with our fingers. This dipping
is not food into food. It is tactile and intimate, a
momentary submersion into a Nile suddenly flowing
red with blood.

We will not partake of our seder feast until we
complete this ritual, because our freedom was
bought with the suffering of the others.

ALL

דָּם	**Dam**
צְפַרְדֵּעַ	**Tz'fardei'a**
כִּנִּים	**Kinim**
עָרוֹב	**Arov**
דֶּבֶר	**Dever**
שְׁחִין	**Sh'chin**
בָּרָד	**Barad**
אַרְבֶּה	**Arbeh**
חֹשֶׁךְ	**Choshech**
מַכַּת בְּכוֹרוֹת	**Makat B'chorot**

Blood, Frogs, Lice, Beasts, Cattle Disease, Boils,
Hail, Locusts, Darkness, Slaying of the First-born.

As we ate our Pascal lambs that last night in Egypt the darkness was pierced with screams. Our door posts were protected by a sign of blood. But from the windows of the Egyptians rose an anguished cry: the death of their first-born.

Yah Sh'chinah, soften our hearts and the hearts of our enemies. Help us to dream new paths to freedom.

So that the next sea-opening is not also a drowning; so that our singing is never again their wailing. So that our freedom leaves no one orphaned, childless, gasping for air.

After the final plague, Pharaoh let the Israelites go. They left Egypt in the middle of the night, and with the full moon as their guide, they walked to the shores of the Red Sea.

According to one *midrash*, they continued to walk until the waters were up to their necks and then— a miracle! The waters parted, and the people crossed on dry land. As Moses and the people rejoiced in song, "…Miriam the Prophet, Aaron's sister, took a timbrel in her hand and all the women went after her with timbrels, dancing" (EXODUS 15:20).

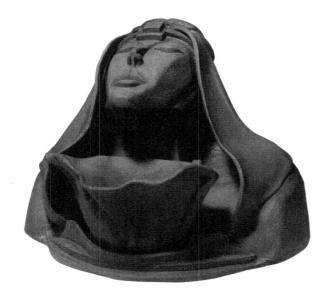

It has become a feminist seder tradition to dance with
tambourines in honor of Miriam's song at the Sea.

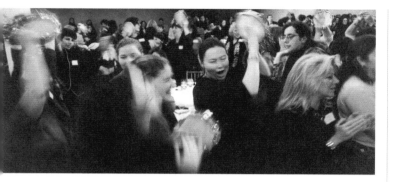

MIRIAM'S SONG

CHORUS:

And the women dancing with their timbrels
Followed Miriam as she sang her song.
Sing a song to the One whom we've exalted.
Miriam and the women danced and danced
the whole night long.

And Miriam was a weaver of unique variety.
The tapestry she wove was one which sang our history.
With every thread and every strand
she crafted her delight.
A woman touched with spirit, she dances
toward the light.
(REPEAT CHORUS)

As Miriam stood upon the shores and gazed
across the sea,
The wonder of this miracle she soon came to believe.
Whoever thought the sea would part with an
outstretched hand,
And we would pass to freedom, and march
to the promised land.
(REPEAT CHORUS)

And Miriam the Prophet took her timbrel in her hand,
And all the women followed her just as
she had planned.
And Miriam raised her voice with song.
She sang with praise and might,
We've just lived through a miracle, we're going
to dance tonight.
(REPEAT CHORUS)

DAYEINU

Ilu hotzi, hotzi'anu
hotzi'anu mimitzrayim (2x) *Dayeinu…*

אִלּוּ הוֹצִיאָנוּ מִמִּצְרַיִם: דַּיֵּנוּ

Ilu natan, natan lanu,
natan lanu, et hashabat. (2x) *Dayeinu…*

אִלּוּ נָתַן לָנוּ אֶת הַשַּׁבָּת: דַּיֵּנוּ

Ilu natan, natan lanu,
natan lanu et hatorah. (2x) *Dayeinu…*

אִלּוּ נָתַן לָנוּ אֶת הַתּוֹרָה: דַּיֵּנוּ

Had God only taken us out of Egypt:
It would have been enough

Had God only given us the Shabbat:
It would have been enough.

Had God only given us the Torah:
It would have been enough.

COMMENTARY

The traditional *Dayeinu* lists God's gifts to the Israelites, beginning with the Exodus and culminating with the Temple in Jerusalem. The refrain of *Dayeinu* is a way of thanking God for each specific step, but also emphasizing how much was given. The interpretive *Dayeinu* that follows changes the focus of action from God to people and from past to present. Like the traditional *Dayeinu*, every step listed is critically important and therefore enough, but also only one part of an ultimate vision of a repaired world, and therefore not enough on its own.

READER

From singing *Dayeinu* we learn to celebrate each landmark on our people's journey. Yet we must never confuse these way stations with the redemptive destination. Because there is still so much to do in our work of repairing the world.

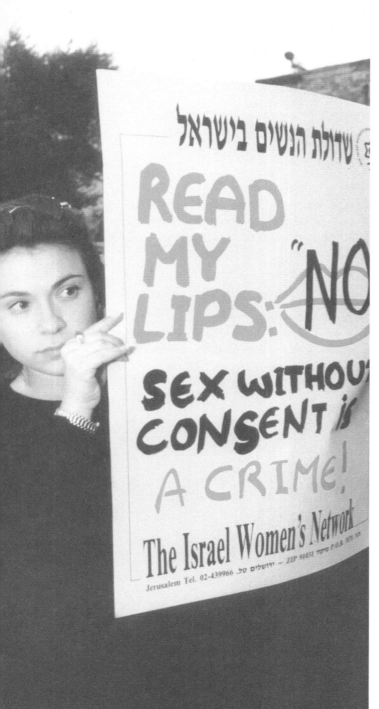

ALL

If we speak truthfully about the pain, joys, and contradictions of our lives,

If we listen to others with sensitivity and compassion,

If we challenge the absence of women in traditional texts, chronicles of Jewish history, and in the leadership of our institutions, *dayeinu*.

If we continue to organize, march, and vote to affirm our values,

If we fight economic injustice, sexism, racism, and homophobia,

If we volunteer our time and money, *dayeinu*.

If we break the silence about violence against women and children in the Jewish community and everywhere,

If we teach our students and children to pursue justice with all their strength,

If we care for the earth and its future as responsibly as we care for those we love,

If we create art, music, dance, and literature, *dayeinu*.

If we realize our power to effect change,

If we bring holiness into our lives, homes, and communities,

If we honor our visions more than our fears, *dayeinu v'lo dayeinu*.

It will and it will not be enough.

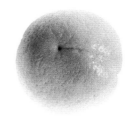

Each of these things can be pointed to or raised when it is mentioned. It is customary not to raise the shankbone because it symbolizes a sacrifice that is no longer offered. According to the Talmud, vegetarians can use a beet instead of a shankbone on the seder plate because it also bleeds. If you have an orange on your seder plate, ask everyone to take a segment of the orange, make the blessing over fruit, and eat it as an act of solidarity with Jewish lesbians and gay men, and others who are marginalized within the Jewish community but whose full integration will ensure a more fruitful future for Judaism. As you eat your orange slice, spit out the seeds as a gesture of repudiating homophobia. (This new ritual was created by Susannah Heschel. See p. 14.)

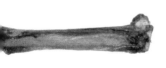

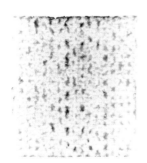

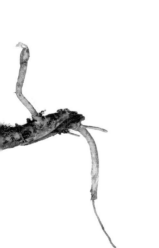

READERS

According to the great sage Rabban Gamliel, those who do not mention three things on Passover do not fulfill their obligation to tell the story: *pesach*, matzah and *maror*.

The *pesach* sacrifice which our ancestors ate while the Temple still stood. Why did they eat it?

Because God passed over (*pasach*) the houses of the Israelites in Egypt while smiting the first born of every Egyptian family.

The matzah, why do we eat this unleavened bread?

Because there was not enough time for our ancestors' dough to rise so they had to bake their unleavened dough into matzah in the desert.

The *maror*, why do we eat these bitter herbs?

Because the Egyptians embittered the Israelites' lives.

Each of these three things, *pesach*, matzah and *maror*, symbolize central aspects of the Passover story. Yet displaying and explaining them does not necessarily ensure the completion of a seder.

ALL

We therefore add to Rabban Gamliel's list that no seder can be complete without the questions of daughters as well as sons and the memory of our mothers as well as our fathers. Thus we sing, "In every generation all of us are obligated to see ourselves as though we personally left Egypt."

בכל דור | B'CHOL DOR

בְּכָל־דּוֹר וָדוֹר חַיָּבִים אָנוּ
לִרְאוֹת אֶת־עַצְמֵנוּ כְּאִלּוּ
כְּאִלּוּ יָצָאנוּ (3x)
מִמִּצְרָיִם

B'chol dor vador chayavim anu
lirot et atzmeinu k'ilu
k'ilu yatzanu (3x)
mi mitzrayim.

In every generation each of us is obligated to see ourselves as if we left Egypt.

COMMENTARY The text of this song closely follows the text in a traditional Haggadah, but it has been reformulated in the plural in order to explicitly include both males and females.

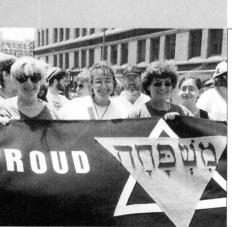

Do Something! Work to make your community and family fully inclusive of gay men, lesbians, bisexuals and transgendered people. Contribute to the Jerusalem Open House, a gay community center in Israel. Contact Keshet to effect concrete changes in your Jewish institutions' GLBT policies and cultures. Donate a copy of *Lesbian Rabbis* or another book by or about gay or lesbian Jews to your synagogue library and invite one of the authors to speak to your community. Challenge language and policies that don't explicitly address the diversity of today's Jewish families.

75

ALL

לְפִיכָךְ אֲנַחְנוּ חַיָּבִים	L'fichach anachnu chayavim
לְהוֹדוֹת לְהַלֵּל לְשַׁבֵּחַ	l'hodot l'haleil l'shabei'ach
לְפָאֵר לְרוֹמֵם לְהַדֵּר	l'fa'eir l'romeim l'hadeir
לְבָרֵךְ לְעַלֵּה וּלְקַלֵּס	l'vareich l'alei ul'kaleis
לְמִי שֶׁעָשָׂה	l'mi she'asta
לַאֲבוֹתֵינוּ וּלְאִמּוֹתֵינוּ וְלָנוּ	la'avoteinu ul'imoteinu v'lanu
אֶת־כָּל־הַנִּסִּים הָאֵלֶּה.	et kol hanisim ha'eileh.
הוֹצִיאָתְנוּ מֵעַבְדוּת לְחֵרוּת	Hotzi'atnu mei'avdut l'cheirut,
מִיָּגוֹן לְשִׂמְחָה מֵאֵבֶל לְיוֹם טוֹב	miyagon l'simcha, mei'eivel l'yom tov,
וּמֵאֲפֵלָה לְאוֹר גָּדוֹל וּמִשִּׁעְבּוּד לִגְאֻלָּה.	umei'afeila l'or gadol, umishibud lig'ula.
וְנֹאמַר לְפָנֶיהָ שִׁירָה חֲדָשָׁה. הַלְלוּיָהּ:	V'nomar l'fanei'ha shira chadasha. Halleluyah.

Therefore we rejoice in our obligation to thank,
sing songs of praise, glorify, exalt, honor, bless, extol,
and lift our voices to the One who is the Source
of miracles for our ancestors and for us. God brought
us forth from slavery to freedom, from sorrow to
joy, from mourning to celebration, from darkness to
great light, from bondage to redemption. Let us
sing a new song. Halleluyah.

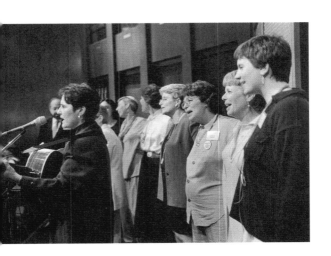

COMMENTARY

The *Hallel* is a special prayer service, composed of excerpts from the Book of Psalms, that is recited on festivals to increase our joy and add more praise of God to our prayers. The word *Hallel* means praise; Halleluyah, which means praise God, uses an ancient name of God, *Yah*, which is grammatically both masculine and feminine.

The following psalm praises God by referring directly to the Exodus. The parts of *Hallel* that refer to future redemption are sung after the meal. All Psalms have been preserved in their original Hebrew.

Sing the first four lines together. The second four lines can be sung as a call and response.

בצאת ישראל

בְּצֵאת יִשְׂרָאֵל מִמִּצְרָיִם בֵּית יַעֲקֹב מֵעַם לֹעֵז:
הָיְתָה יְהוּדָה לְקָדְשׁוֹ יִשְׂרָאֵל מַמְשְׁלוֹתָיו:
הַיָּם רָאָה וַיָּנֹס הַיַּרְדֵּן יִסֹּב לְאָחוֹר:
הֶהָרִים רָקְדוּ כְאֵילִים גְּבָעוֹת כִּבְנֵי־צֹאן:
מַה־לְּךָ הַיָּם כִּי תָנוּס הַיַּרְדֵּן תִּסֹּב לְאָחוֹר:
הֶהָרִים תִּרְקְדוּ כְאֵילִים גְּבָעוֹת כִּבְנֵי־צֹאן:
מִלִּפְנֵי אָדוֹן חוּלִי אָרֶץ מִלִּפְנֵי אֱלוֹהַּ יַעֲקֹב:
הַהֹפְכִי הַצּוּר אֲגַם־מָיִם חַלָּמִישׁ לְמַעְיְנוֹ מָיִם:

B'TZEIT YISRAEIL (PSALM 114)

B'tzeit yisraeil mimitzrayim beit ya'akov mei'am lo'eiz.
Hay'ta y'huda l'kodsho yisraeil mamsh'lotav.
Hayam ra'a vayanos hayardein yisov l'achor.
Heharim rak'du ch'eilim g'va'ot kivnei tzon.
Ma l'cha hayam ki tanus hayardein tisov l'achor.
Heharim tirk'du ch'eilim g'va'ot kivnei tzon.
Milifnei adon chuli aretz milifnei elo'ah ya'akov.
Hahofchi hatzur agam mayim chalamish l'may'no mayim.

When Israel went out of Egypt, when the house of Jacob emerged from a babel of tongues, Judah became God's dwelling place, Israel, God's dominion. The sea looked and fled, the Jordan turned back. The mountains danced like lambs, the hills like young sheep. Why do you flee, O sea? O Jordan, why do you change your course? Why do you frolic, O mountains? Why do the hills tremble? In God's presence, the earth moves before the God of Jacob. You transform rocks into pools of water, You turn flint into flowing springs.

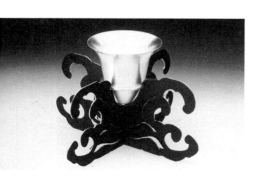

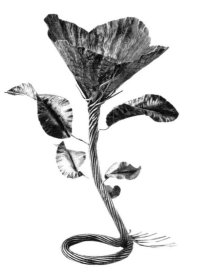

READERS

וְהִצַּלְתִּי אֶתְכֶם מֵעֲבֹדָתָם   V'hitzalti etchem mei'avodatam

"I will deliver you from under their bondage"
(EXODUS 6:6).

The second cup recalls God's promise to deliver the slaves from their bondage. With this cup, we honor women who used their own experiences of the "narrow places" to empower others to deliver themselves from bondage.

We dedicate this cup to: Glikl of Hameln, Pauline Newman, Rose Schneiderman, Lillian Wald, Manya Wilbushewitch Shochat.

Invite people around the table to add names of women to honor with this cup. Select and read a biography of one of these women from Appendix I. Alternatively, choose a woman from your own family or community and share her story.

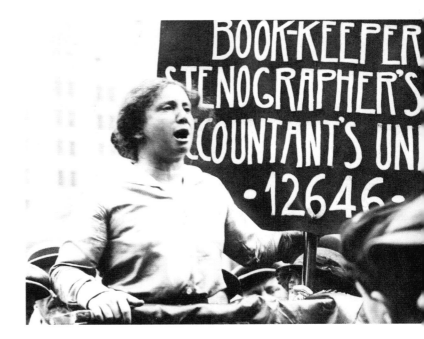

Lift the cup and recite the blessing.

בְּרוּכָה אַתְּ יָהּ אֱלֹהֵינוּ רוּחַ הָעוֹלָם
בּוֹרֵאת פְּרִי הַגָּפֶן.

B'rucha at yah eloheinu ruach ha'olam
boreit p'ri hagafen.

or

בָּרוּךְ אַתָּה יְיָ אֱלֹהֵינוּ מֶלֶךְ הָעוֹלָם
בּוֹרֵא פְּרִי הַגָּפֶן.

Baruch atah adonai eloheinu melech ha'olam
borei p'ri hagafen.

You are Blessed, Our God, Spirit of the World,
who creates the fruit of the vine.

Drink the second cup.

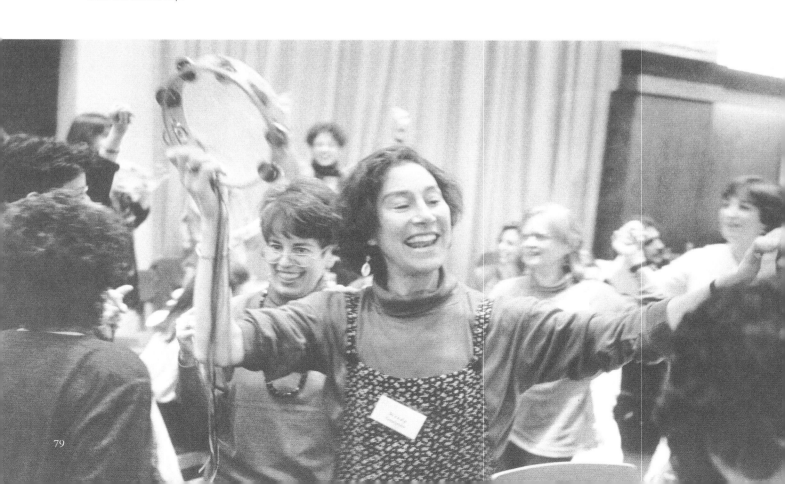

79

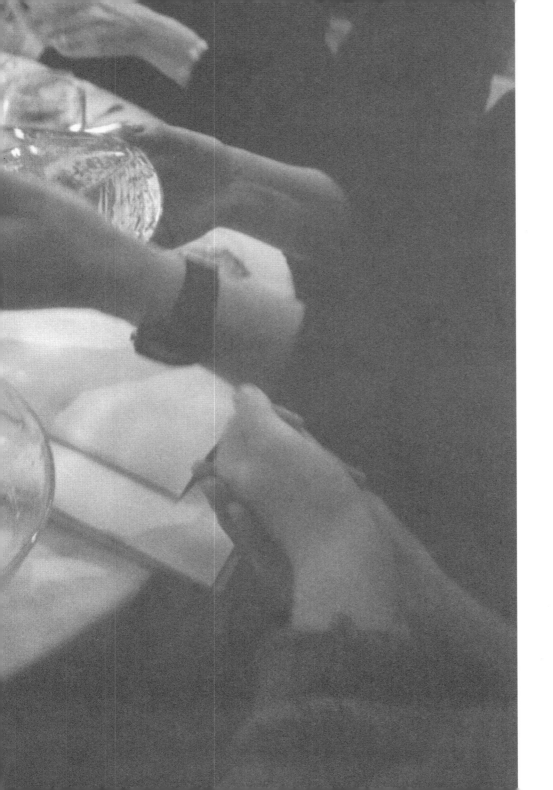

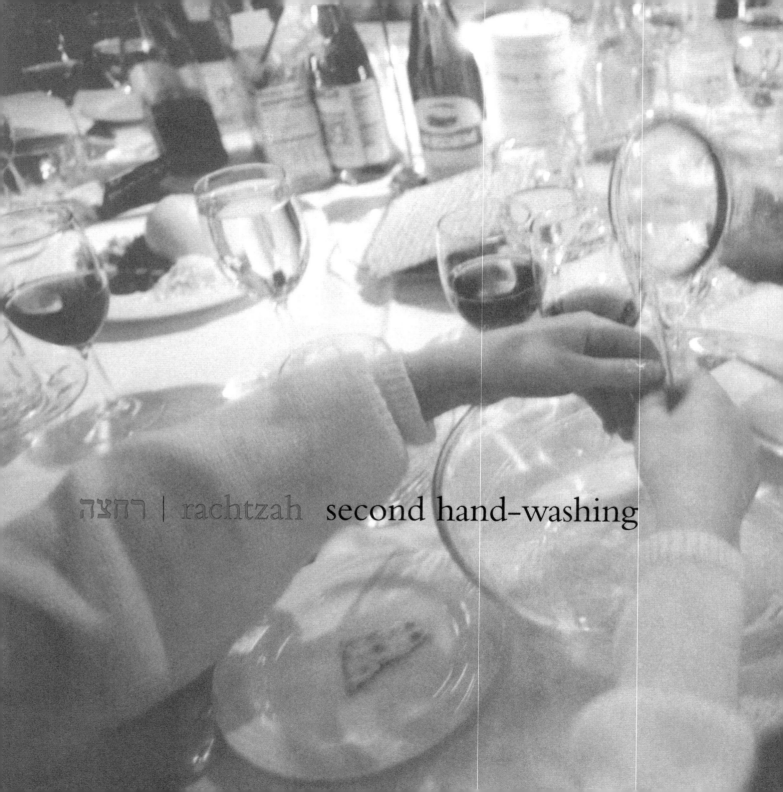

רחצה | rachtzah   second hand-washing

Wash your hands, this time following the hand-washing with the blessing below. Because the act of washing is linked to the act of eating, it is customary to refrain from speaking between the hand-washing blessing and the blessings over the bread. Use the time it takes for everyone to wash her hands as an opportunity for contemplative silence or sing a *niggun*. Then continue with the hand-washing blessing followed by the two matzah blessings.

בְּרוּכָה אַתְּ יָהּ אֱלֹהֵינוּ רוּחַ הָעוֹלָם
אֲשֶׁר קִדְּשַׁתְנוּ בְּמִצְוֹתֶיהָ וְצִוַּתְנוּ
עַל נְטִילַת יָדָיִם:

בָּרוּךְ אַתָּה יְיָ אֱלֹהֵינוּ מֶלֶךְ הָעוֹלָם
אֲשֶׁר קִדְּשָׁנוּ בְּמִצְוֹתָיו וְצִוָּנוּ
עַל נְטִילַת יָדָיִם:

B'rucha at yah eloheinu ruach ha'olam
asher kidshatnu b'mitzvoteha v'tzivatnu
al n'tilat yadayim.

or

Baruch atah adonai eloheinu melech ha'olam
asher kidshanu b'mitzvotav v'tzivanu
al n'tilat yadayim.

You are Blessed, Our God, Spirit of the World, who makes us holy with *mitzvot* and commands us to wash our hands.

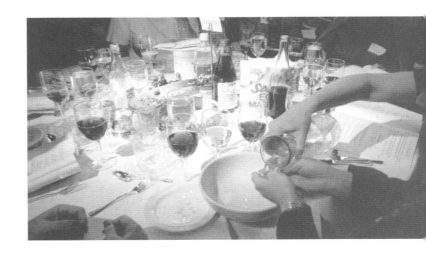

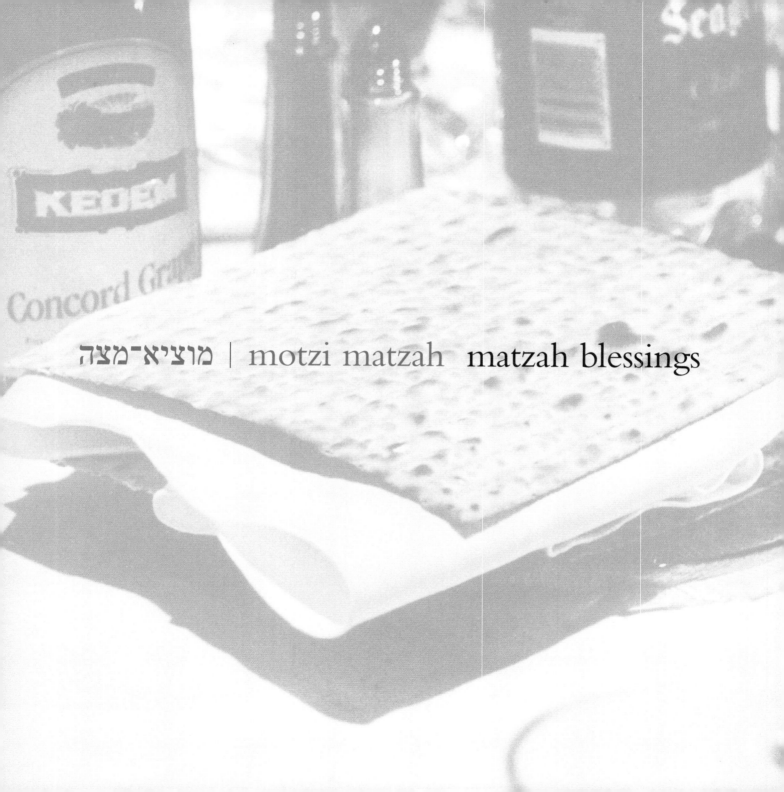

מוֹצִיא־מַצָּה | motzi matzah   matzah blessings

Raise all three *matzot*, and say the first of the two
blessings over the matzah.

בְּרוּכָה אַתְּ יָהּ אֱלֹהֵינוּ רוּחַ הָעוֹלָם
הַמּוֹצִיאָה לֶחֶם מִן הָאָרֶץ.

B'rucha at yah eloheinu ruach ha'olam

hamotzi'a lechem min ha'aretz.

or

בָּרוּךְ אַתָּה יְיָ אֱלֹהֵינוּ מֶלֶךְ הָעוֹלָם
הַמּוֹצִיא לֶחֶם מִן הָאָרֶץ.

Baruch atah adonai eloheinu melech ha'olam

hamotzi lechem min ha'aretz.

You are Blessed, Our God, Spirit of the World,
who brings forth bread from the earth.

Put down the bottom matzah, lift the broken middle one with
the top one, and say the second matzah blessing. After the
blessing, eat the matzah. Everyone should get at least a small
piece of the top matzah and the broken middle matzah.

בְּרוּכָה אַתְּ יָהּ אֱלֹהֵינוּ רוּחַ הָעוֹלָם
אֲשֶׁר קִדְּשַׁתְנוּ בְּמִצְוֹתֶיהָ וְצִוַּתְנוּ
עַל אֲכִילַת מַצָּה:

B'rucha at yah eloheinu ruach ha'olam

asher kidshatnu b'mitzvoteha v'tzivatnu

al achilat matzah.

or

בָּרוּךְ אַתָּה יְיָ אֱלֹהֵינוּ מֶלֶךְ הָעוֹלָם
אֲשֶׁר קִדְּשָׁנוּ בְּמִצְוֹתָיו וְצִוָּנוּ
עַל אֲכִילַת מַצָּה:

Baruch atah adonai eloheinu melech ha'olam

asher kidshanu b'mitzvotav v'tzivanu

al achilat matzah.

You are Blessed, Our God, Spirit of the World,
who makes us holy with *mitzvot* and commands
us to eat matzah.

COMMENTARY   Each of the two blessings over the matzah serve a different purpose.
The first blessing is recited over the matzah as bread. The second blessing
is recited specifically for the *mitzvah* of eating matzah on the seder nights.

מרור | maror   bitter herbs

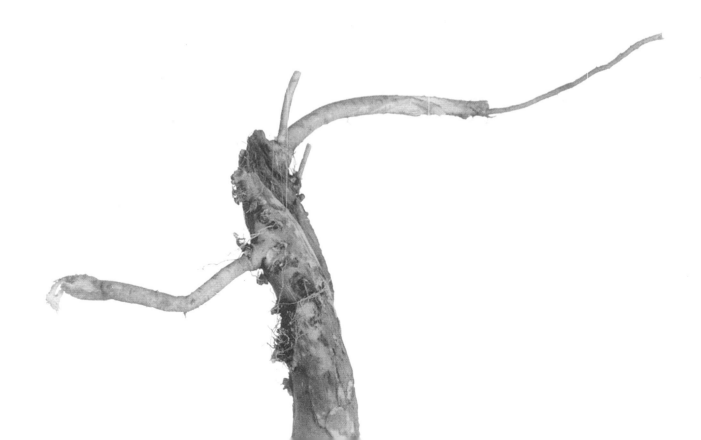

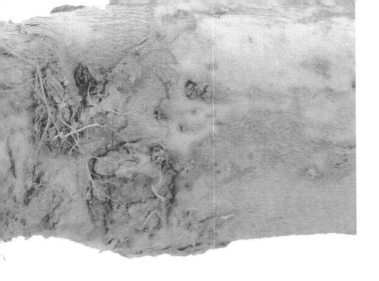

This is the way to experience bitterness: take a big chunk of raw horseradish, let the burning turn your face all red.

This is the way to experience bitterness: dig back to a time of raw wounds, remember how it felt before the healing began, years or months or days ago.

This is the way to experience bitterness: hold the hand of a friend in pain, listen to her story, remember Naomi who renamed herself Mara, bitterness, because she "went away full but God brought [her] back empty" (RUTH 1:21).

This is the way to experience bitterness: recall the pain of exclusion that is part of the legacy of Jewish women. Listen to the words of Bertha Pappenheim, founder of the German Jewish feminist movement, who said, "No continuing education can repair how the souls of Jewish women—and thus Judaism in its entirety—have been sinned against…"

Or the words of Henrietta Szold, founder of Hadassah, who wrote, "But do not speak to me of the progressiveness of Judaism! Why isn't there one prayer in all the books to fit my modern case— not one to raise up the spirit of the so-called emancipated woman?"

How big a piece of *maror* must we eat to re-experience this bitterness?

And what if I've known enough pain this year already? And what if exclusion is not just a memory for me?

And what if I eat the whole root and my tongue catches on fire and my ears burn? Then will I know slavery?

בְּרוּכָה אַתְּ יָהּ אֱלֹהֵינוּ רוּחַ הָעוֹלָם
אֲשֶׁר קִדְּשַׁתְנוּ בְּמִצְוֹתֶיהָ וְצִוַּתְנוּ
עַל אֲכִילַת מָרוֹר:

B'rucha at yah eloheinu ruach ha'olam
asher kid'shatnu b'mitzvoteha v'tzivatnu
al achilat maror.

or

בָּרוּךְ אַתָּה יְיָ אֱלֹהֵינוּ מֶלֶךְ הָעוֹלָם
אֲשֶׁר קִדְּשָׁנוּ בְּמִצְוֹתָיו וְצִוָּנוּ
עַל אֲכִילַת מָרוֹר:

Baruch atah adonai eloheinu melech ha'olam
asher kid'shanu b'mitzvotav v'tzivanu
al achilat maror.

You are Blessed, Our God, Spirit of the World, who makes us holy with *mitzvot* and commands us to eat bitter herbs.

Eat the *maror* but do not recline, because *maror* is a symbol of slavery and reclining is a posture of freedom. Some eat the horseradish plain, others eat it dipped in *charoset*.

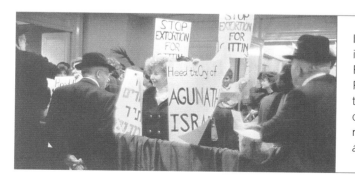

Do Something! Help end the bitterness of domestic violence in Jewish women's lives by supporting the Association of Rape Crisis Centers in Israel and the Center for the Prevention of Sexual and Domestic Violence in Seattle. Call the Jewish Orthodox Feminist Alliance to find out how you can support *agunot*, Jewish women whose husbands have refused to give them a *get*, a Jewish bill of divorce. Support *agunot* in Israel through *Mavoi Satum*.

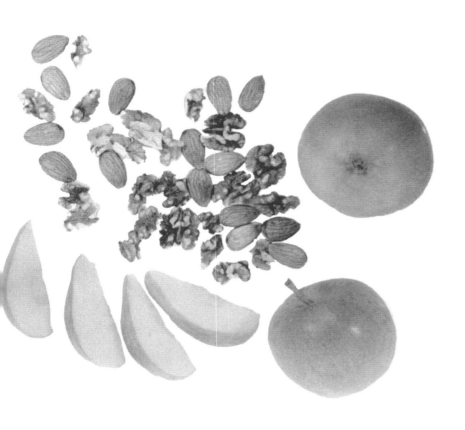

כורך | korech hillel sandwich

Make a sandwich using a piece of the bottom of the three ceremonial *matzot*, other matzah as needed and another piece of *maror*. Many also add *charoset* to the sandwich. Eat the sandwich.

COMMENTARY

The second-century sage Hillel interpreted the biblical commandment to eat the *pesach*, matzah, and *maror* as a commandment to eat all three mixed together instead of one at a time. Thus, during the time of the Temple, he ate a sandwich of roasted lamb, matzah and *maror*. Our own sandwich, lacking the meat of a *pesach* sacrifice, combines the symbols of slavery with the symbols of freedom by mixing *maror* with matzah and *charoset*.

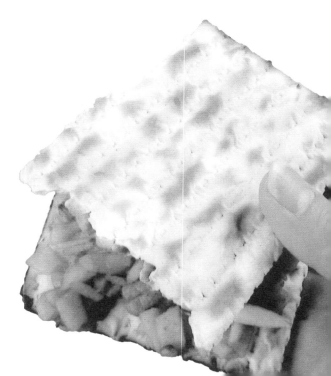

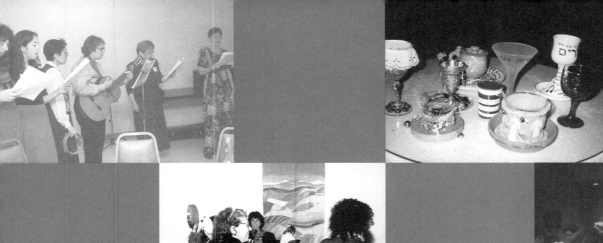

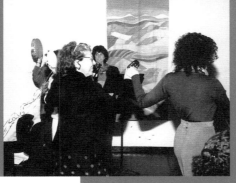

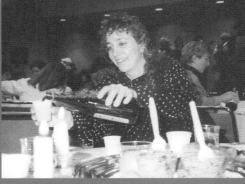

שולחן עורך   shulchan oreich   the festive meal

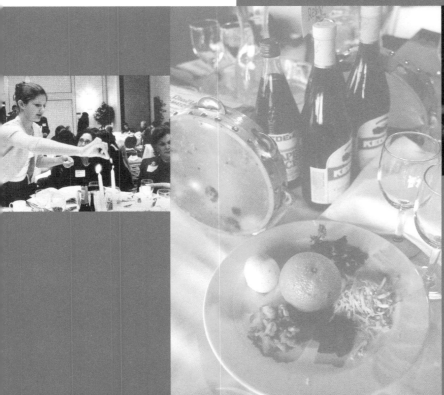

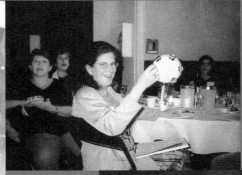

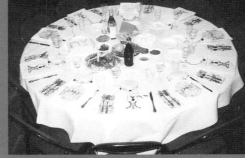

It is customary in many communities to begin the meal with hard-boiled eggs, usually dipped in salt-water.

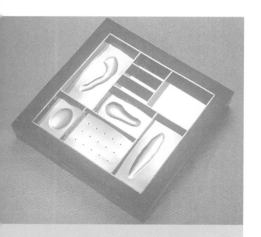

COMMENTARY

There are multiple interpretations for the custom of beginning the meal with a hard-boiled egg. Eggs represent the renewal of spring and the rebirth of the Jewish people. A roasted egg is also a reminder of the sacrifice which took place in the Temple. As hard-boiled eggs are also the first foods eaten by mourners after a burial, they are also associated with mourning, perhaps for the loss of the Temple.

צפון | tzafun   retrieving the hidden matzah

To conclude the meal, retrieve the *afikomen*, the hidden broken half of the middle matzah, and distribute a small piece to each person. Each person eats a small piece of the *afikomen* as a sign that the meal has concluded.

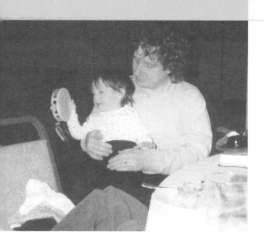

COMMENTARY

Afikomen customs vary. At some seders, children "steal" the *afikomen* during the meal and hide it from the seder leader(s) who offer(s) "ransom" in the form of gifts or pledges in exchange for its retrieval. At other seders, the seder leader(s) hide the *afikomen* and the children look for it. When the children find it they bargain for gifts in exchange for it. Seders without children can still partake in this ritual treasure hunt. For both adults and children, gifts of *tzedakah* given in honor of the holders of the *afikomen* to projects of their choosing are a good idea.

READERS

"So, who has found the *afikomen*?" we ask. The finders hold the napkin-covered matzah tightly in their hands and are determined to bargain.

It is a part of our lesson plan—this small rebellion. Each year we teach a new generation to resist bondage, to envision someplace better, to savor freedom, and to take responsibility for the journeys of their lives.

And each year with the *afikomen* ritual, they hold power in their hands, just long enough to say, "Yes" or "No," with all eyes on them. With people waiting.

"We can't finish the seder without it."

Just long enough to learn to ask for what they want.

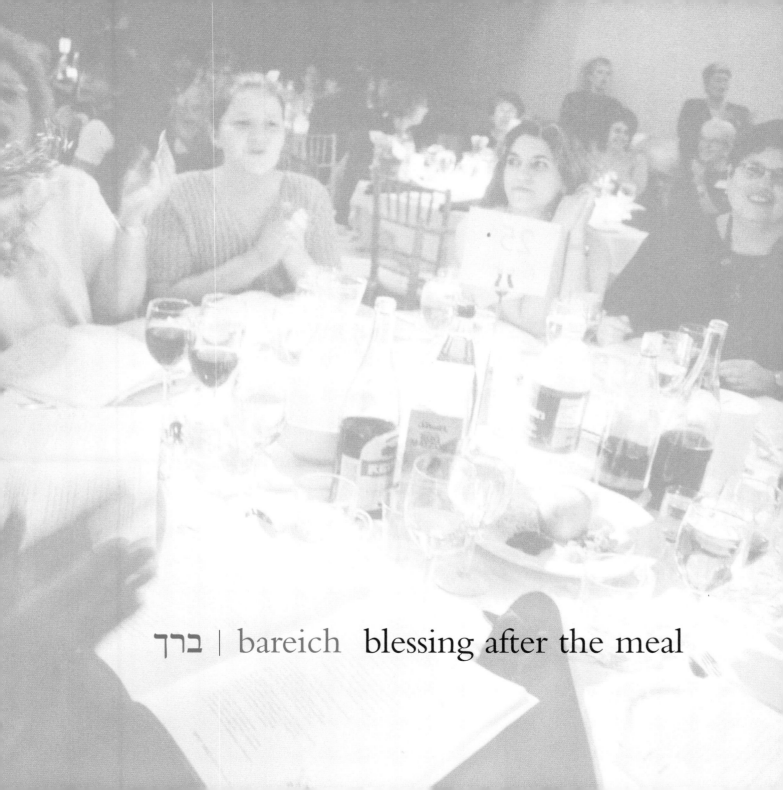

ברך | bareich blessing after the meal

Pour the third cup. Before the blessing after the meal, take a moment to acknowledge and thank all those responsible for preparing the meal just completed. Recite the names of all who were involved in cleaning the kitchen, purchasing the food, cooking, baking, serving, and washing dishes. In their honor recite the following verse from the Book of Proverbs, 31:31.

For a woman:

תְּנוּ-לָהּ מִפְּרִי יָדֶיהָ וִיהַלְלוּהָ
בַשְּׁעָרִים מַעֲשֶׂיהָ:

T'nu la mipri yadeiha v'yihalleluha
vash'arim ma'asei'ha

Give her of the fruit of her hands; and let her own deeds praise her in the gates.

For a man:

תְּנוּ-לוֹ מִפְּרִי יָדָיו וִיהַלְלוּהוּ
בַשְּׁעָרִים מַעֲשָׂיו

T'nu lo mipri yadav v'yihalleluhu
vash'arim ma'asav

Give him of the fruit of his hands; and let his own deeds praise him in the gates. (adapted)

On the first two nights of Passover and Shabbat, begin the Blessings After the Meal with Psalm 126. Then continue either with the creative, mostly English, blessings on pages 97-99, or with the tradtional blessings in Appendix I pages 113-121.

שיר המעלות

SHIR HAMA'ALOT

שִׁיר הַמַּעֲלוֹת בְּשׁוּב יְיָ
אֶת־שִׁיבַת צִיּוֹן הָיִינוּ כְּחֹלְמִים.
אָז יִמָּלֵא שְׂחוֹק פִּינוּ וּלְשׁוֹנֵנוּ רִנָּה.
אָז יֹאמְרוּ בַגּוֹיִם
הִגְדִּיל יְיָ לַעֲשׂוֹת עִם־אֵלֶּה.
הִגְדִּיל יְיָ לַעֲשׂוֹת עִמָּנוּ הָיִינוּ שְׂמֵחִים.
שׁוּבָה יְיָ אֶת־שְׁבִיתֵנוּ כַּאֲפִיקִים בַּנֶּגֶב.
הַזֹּרְעִים בְּדִמְעָה בְּרִנָּה יִקְצֹרוּ.
הָלוֹךְ יֵלֵךְ וּבָכֹה נֹשֵׂא מֶשֶׁךְ־הַזָּרַע
בֹּא־יָבֹא בְרִנָּה נֹשֵׂא אֲלֻמֹּתָיו.

Shir hama'alot, b'shuv adonai
et shivat tzi'yon, hayinu k'cholmim.
Az yimalei s'chok pinu ulshoneinu rina.
Az yomru vagoyim,
hig'dil adonai la'asot im eileh.
Hig'dil adonai la'asot imanu hayinu s'meichim.
Shuva adonai et sh'viteinu ka'afikim banegev.
Hazor'im b'dim'a b'rina yik'tzoru.
Haloch yei'leich 'uvacho nosei meshech hazara
bo'yavo v'rina nosei alumotav.

A Song of Ascents. When God restores the scattered ones of Zion, it will be the fulfillment of a dream. Our mouths will be filled with laughter then; our tongues with song. Then the nations will say: "God has done great things for them." God has done great things for us. We rejoice. Carry our captives back, O God, like water coursing through a dry riverbed. Those who sow in tears will reap in joy. Those who plant in sorrow will return with song, sheaves piled high.

COMMENTARY

The following text incorporates the themes and core phrases of the traditional Hebrew blessing after the meal. In this case, to accommodate the rhyme and verse, some of the Hebrew retains its traditional masculine formulation.

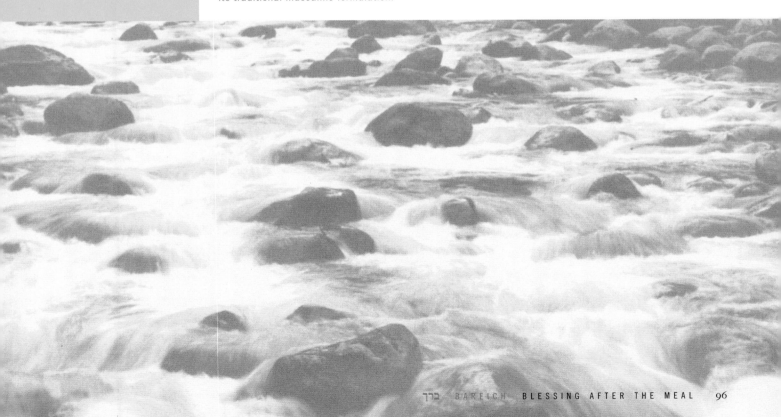

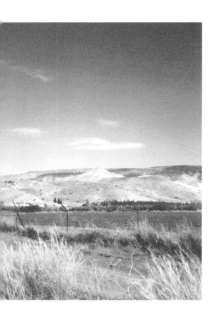

ברכת המזון   BIRKAT HAMAZON

We bless You God
You have nourished all the world
With goodness, graciousness and kindness
May You give food and life to every living thing
May we all learn to do the same
And so we thank the One
Who gives us food for life
May we provide for every living soul.
Baruch atah adonai hazan et hakol.

בָּרוּךְ אַתָּה יְיָ הַזָּן אֶת־הַכֹּל.

We thank You, God, for the legacy we share
For the rich fertile land that we inherit
For the gift of freedom, of Torah, and of life
Every day, every season, every hour
You give us food to live
You give us strength to give
Every day, every moment with *b'racha*
nodeh lach, nodeh l'cha
We say
toda raba b'chol eit uv'chol sha'a.

נוֹדֶה לָךְ נוֹדֶה לְךָ

תּוֹדָה רַבָּה בְּכָל־עֵת וּבְכָל־שָׁעָה.

Kakatuv,
It is written in Torah
You will eat, you will drink and you'll be sated
Then you will bless the One
Who has given you this world
Who has filled it with beauty and with life
We'll guard this earth, these lands
The torrent seas and sands
All the seeds that we have not yet sown
For land so rich and full
We give our thanks to You
Al ha'aretz v'al hamazon.

כַּכָּתוּב

עַל־הָאָרֶץ וְעַל־הַמָּזוֹן.

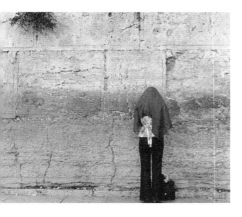

O You, the God of our present and our past
Please remember those who came before us
And care for us as we pray for
Y'rushalayim
The city of wholeness and peace.

יְרוּשָׁלָיִם

We ask that we be blessed
With everything that's good
That every blessing make our lives more whole
That every one of us
Be strengthened by Your light
Bakol, mi'kol, kol.

בַּכֹּל מִכֹּל כֹּל.

O, Source of compassion,
Through the ages we've been blessed
May we build this city of peace
And may all people make it a place of
peace and freedom
In our day, now, the time has come
We bless the Source of all
Who builds Jerusalem
With compassion in our day
Boneh v'rachamav y'rushalayim amen.

בּוֹנֶה בְרַחֲמָיו יְרוּשָׁלָיִם אָמֵן:

We bless You, O God,
who has taught us what is good
Heiteev, meiteev, yeiteev
You have sustained us and
blessed us now and at all times
Chein vachesed v'rachamim.

הֵטִיב מֵטִיב יֵיטִיב

חֵן וָחֶסֶד וְרַחֲמִים.

Harachaman, Your love surrounds us
now and forever more.
Harachaman, bring truth and justice
to Heaven and to Earth.

הָרַחֲמָן

Harachaman, all generations will
glorify and praise You.
Harachaman, You give us honor,
may we live with dignity.
Harachaman, You give us freedom,
may we help those imprisoned.
Harachaman, here at this table,
we nourish one and all.
Harachaman, bless us with vision,
a better world we promise.
Harachaman, the One of Mercy,
be with us, *Harachaman*.

On Shabbat add:

Harachaman, the One of Mercy,
You give rest and comfort.
Harachaman, the One of Mercy,
from now to eternity.

On holidays add:

Harachaman, the One of Mercy,
You give us days of goodness.
Harachaman, the One of Mercy,
You give us sacred times.

עֹשֶׂה שָׁלוֹם בִּמְרוֹמָיו
הוּא יַעֲשֶׂה שָׁלוֹם עָלֵינוּ
וְעַל־כָּל־יִשְׂרָאֵל וְעַל־כָּל־יוֹשְׁבֵי תֵבֵל
וְאִמְרוּ אָמֵן:

*Oseh shalom bimromav
hu ya'aseh shalom aleinu
v'al kol yisraeil, v'al kol yoshvei teiveil,
v'im'ru amen.*

כוס שלישי KOS SHLISHI THIRD CUP

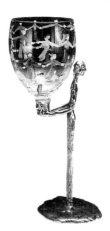

וְגָאַלְתִּי אֶתְכֶם בִּזְרוֹעַ נְטוּיָה וּבִשְׁפָטִים גְּדֹלִים

Invite people around the table to add names of women to honor with this cup. Select and read a biography of one of these women from Appendix I. Alternatively, choose a woman from your own family or community and share her story. Lift the cup and recite the blessing.

בְּרוּכָה אַתְּ יָהּ אֱלֹהֵינוּ רוּחַ הָעוֹלָם
בּוֹרֵאת פְּרִי הַגָּפֶן.

בָּרוּךְ אַתָּה יְיָ אֱלֹהֵינוּ מֶלֶךְ הָעוֹלָם
בּוֹרֵא פְּרִי הַגָּפֶן.

Drink the third cup while reclining on the left side and then fill the fourth cup.

READERS

V'ga'alti etchem bizro'a n'tuya uvish'fatim g'dolim

"And I will redeem you with an outstretched arm and with great judgments" (EXODUS 6:6).

The third cup we drink tonight is linked to the verse from Exodus which tells of God's promise to redeem Israel with an outstretched arm and with great judgments. As the "outstretched arm" is a manifestation of God's power, we recall now Jewish women who used their power and strength to make real this Divine promise of redemption. We dedicate this cup to: Henrietta Szold, Rachel Kagan, Justine Wise Polier, Bella Abzug.

B'rucha at yah eloheinu ruach ha'olam
boreit p'ri hagafen.

or

Baruch atah adonai eloheinu melech ha'olam
borei p'ri hagafen.

You are Blessed, Our God, Spirit of the World,
who creates the fruit of the vine.

100

At this point in the seder Jewish communities, beset by persecution during the Crusades, opened their doors and recited the angry plea *Sh'foch Chamat'cha...* "Pour out Your wrath upon the nations who do not know You."

In other communities during the same period, the hope for redemption was so intense that families sang to invoke the Prophet Elijah who, according to legend, would herald an era of Messianic peace, justice, and healing.

We open our doors now with the need to act on both impulses. The crimes of humanity that we continue to see—mass rape and torture, ethnic cleansing, the destruction of entire cities and cultures—cry out for just retribution beyond our limited capacity. And our longings for peace, for healing of earth, body and spirit, still bring the hope-drenched melody of *Eiliyahu Hanavi* to our lips.

With that melody we bridge our hopes for the future with our commitment to the present. We thus invite to our seders not just Elijah, harbinger of the Messiah, but Miriam, inspiration for the journey.

Open, or turn towards the door, rise and sing. Use the same melody for "*Eiliyahu Hanavi*" and "*Mir'yam Han'via.*"

EILIYAHU HANAVI

אֵלִיָּהוּ הַנָּבִיא

אֵלִיָּהוּ הַנָּבִיא אֵלִיָּהוּ הַתִּשְׁבִּי
אֵלִיָּהוּ אֵלִיָּהוּ אֵלִיָּהוּ הַגִּלְעָדִי
בִּמְהֵרָה בְיָמֵינוּ יָבוֹא אֵלֵינוּ
עִם מָשִׁיחַ בֶּן דָּוִד:

Eiliyahu hanavi, eiliyahu hatishbi,
Eiliyahu, eiliyahu, eiliyahu hagiladi.
Bimheira v'yameinu, yavo eileinu,
im mashiach ben david. (2x)

Elijah the Prophet, come to us soon,
for you herald Messianic days.

MIR'YAM HAN'VI'A

מרים הנביאה

מִרְיָם הַנְּבִיאָה עֹז וְזִמְרָה בְּיָדָהּ.
מִרְיָם תִּרְקוֹד אִתָּנוּ לְהַגְדִּיל זִמְרַת עוֹלָם.
מִרְיָם תִּרְקוֹד אִתָּנוּ לְתַקֵּן אֶת־הָעוֹלָם.
בִּמְהֵרָה בְיָמֵינוּ הִיא תְּבִיאֵנוּ
אֶל מֵי הַיְשׁוּעָה אֶל מֵי הַיְשׁוּעָה:

Mir'yam han'vi'a oz v'zimra b'yada.
Mir'yam, tirkod itanu, l'hagdil zimrat olam.
Mir'yam, tirkod itanu, l'takein et ha'olam.
Bim'heira v'yameinu, hi t'vi'einu.
El mei ha'y'shua. El mei ha'y'shua.

Miriam the Prophet, strength and song are in her hand. Miriam will dance with us to strengthen the world's song. Miriam will dance with us to heal the world. Soon, and in our time, she will lead us to the waters of salvation.

Close the door and be seated.

Do Something! Support women working for peace and social change around the world. Contact the Women's Empowerment Fund of the American World Jewish Service to find out how you can be involved in supporting women activists in developing countries. Support Project Kesher in their work to empower Jewish women of the former Soviet Union. Tell high school girls in your community about Seeking Common Ground, a peace and leadership development program that brings together Palestinian, Israeli, and American high school women.

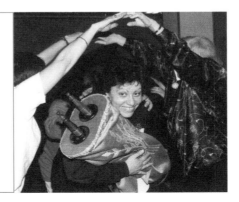

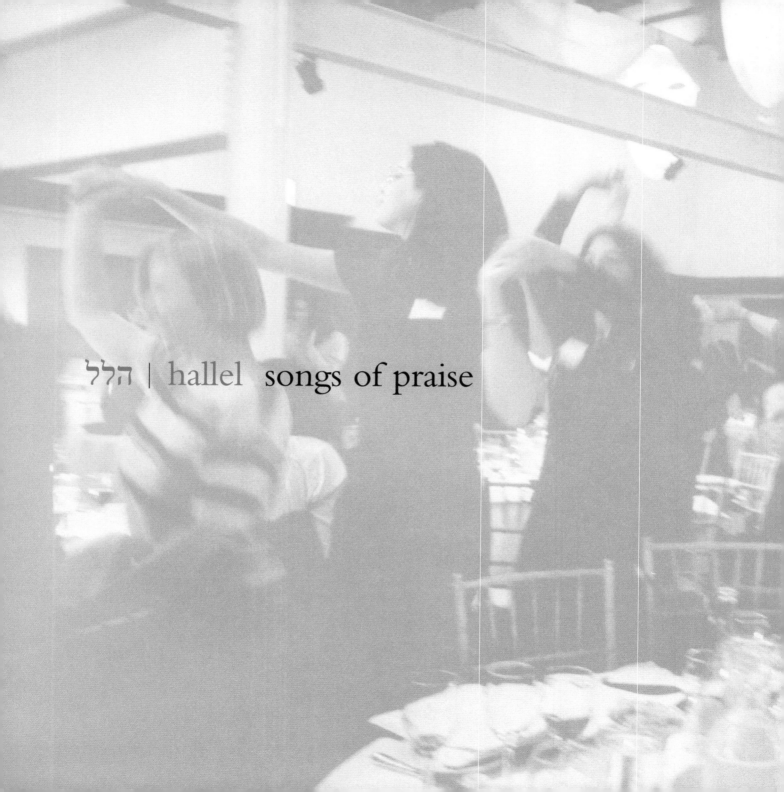

הלל | hallel songs of praise

מן המצר | MIN HAMEITZAR (PSALM 118:5)

מִן־הַמֵּצַר קָרָאתִי יָהּ | *Min hameitzar karati yah*
עָנָנִי בַמֶּרְחָב יָהּ: | *anani vamerchav yah*
עָנָנִי | *anani* (3x)
בַמֶּרְחָב יָהּ: | *vamerchav yah.*

From a narrow place, I cried out to God.
God answered me with wide expanse.

Though we began Hallel before the meal we conclude it now.

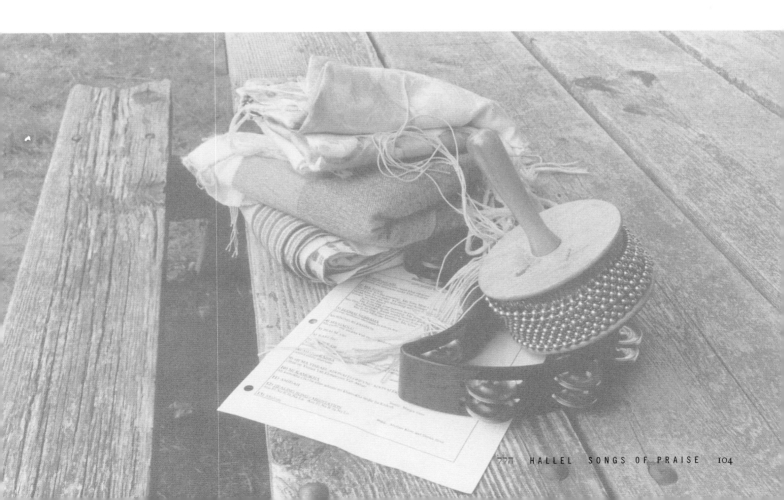

הַלְלוּיָהּ.	*Hal'lu'yah.* (4x)
הַלְלוּ אֵל־בְּקָדְשׁוֹ	*Hal'lu eil b'kodsho,*
הַלְלוּהוּ בִּרְקִיעַ עֻזּוֹ:	*hal'luhu birki'a uzo.*
הַלְלוּהוּ בִגְבוּרֹתָיו	*Hal'luhu bigvurotav,*
הַלְלוּהוּ כְּרֹב גֻּדְלוֹ:	*hal'luhu k'rov gud'lo.*
הַלְלוּיָהּ.	*Hal'lu'yah.* (4x)
הַלְלוּהוּ בְּתֵקַע שׁוֹפָר	*Hal'luhu b'teika shofar,*
הַלְלוּהוּ בְּנֵבֶל וְכִנּוֹר:	*hal'luhu b'neivel v'chinor.*
הַלְלוּהוּ בְתֹף וּמָחוֹל	*Hal'luhu b'tof umachol,*
הַלְלוּהוּ בְּמִנִּים וְעֻגָב:	*hal'luhu b'minim v'ugav.*
הַלְלוּיָהּ.	*Hal'lu'yah.* (4x)
הַלְלוּהוּ בְצִלְצְלֵי־שָׁמַע	*Hal'luhu b'tziltz'lei shama,*
הַלְלוּהוּ בְּצִלְצְלֵי תְרוּעָה:	*hal'luhu b'tziltz'lei t'rua.*
כֹּל הַנְּשָׁמָה תְּהַלֵּל יָהּ.	*Kol han'shama t'haleil yah.*
כֹּל הַנְּשָׁמָה תְּהַלֵּל יָהּ.	*Kol han'shama t'haleil yah.*
הַלְלוּיָהּ.	*Hal'lu'yah.* (4x)

Halleluyah! Praise God in God's sanctuary;
Praise God whose power the heavens proclaim.
Praise God for mighty acts;
Praise God for surpassing greatness.
Praise God with shofar blast;
Praise God with harp and lute.
Praise God with drum and dance;
Praise God with strings and pipe.
Praise God with cymbals sounding;
Praise God with cymbals resounding.
Let every soul praise God. Halleluyah!

Include Counting the Omer on the second night
of Passover or any night following.

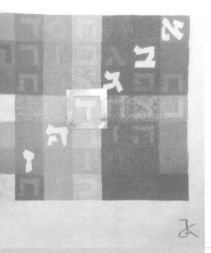

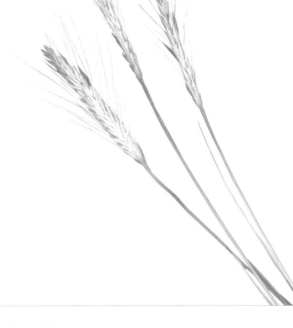

COMMENTARY

In Leviticus 23, we are told to bring the first sheaf of the harvest, known as
the *Omer*, as a wave-offering to the priest at the Temple on the second day
of Passover. From that day, we are to count seven weeks. The fiftieth day
is a holy gathering, unnamed in the Torah, but now celebrated as the holiday
of *Shavuot*, which according to tradition, is when the Jewish people received
the Torah at Sinai.

The period of forty-nine days between Passover and Shavuot is known as
the *Omer* and each day is marked by a blessing and a counting of the *Omer*.
The Kabbalists saw the *Omer* as a period of preparation and ascent, a
climbing of 49 rungs of a ladder to reach a state of purity, so that by the
50th day, as we reach the summit, we have made ourselves ready to receive
the Torah. The first opportunity to count the *Omer* comes towards the end
of the second seder, letting us know that even as we near completion of one
ritual, another is beginning. Just as we begin to comprehend what it means
to re-experience leaving Egypt, we are presented with the challenge of
preparing for revelation at Sinai.

Recite the blessing for counting the *Omer* and then continue
with the appropriate phrase stating which day of the *Omer*
is being counted.

בְּרוּכָה אַתְּ יָהּ אֱלֹהֵינוּ רוּחַ הָעוֹלָם
אֲשֶׁר קִדְּשַׁתְנוּ בְּמִצְוֹתֶיהָ וְצִוַּתְנוּ
עַל סְפִירַת הָעֹמֶר:

B'rucha at yah eloheinu ruach ha'olam
asher kid'shatnu b'mitzvoteha v'tzivatnu
al s'firat ha'omer.

or

בָּרוּךְ אַתָּה יְיָ אֱלֹהֵינוּ מֶלֶךְ הָעוֹלָם
אֲשֶׁר קִדְּשָׁנוּ בְּמִצְוֹתָיו וְצִוָּנוּ
עַל סְפִירַת הָעֹמֶר:

Baruch atah adonai eloheinu melech ha'olam
asher kid'shanu b'mitzvotav v'tzivanu
al s'firat ha'omer.

You are blessed, Our God, Spirit of the
World, who makes us holy with *mitzvot* and
commands us to count the *Omer*.

For the first day of the *Omer* which begins on the second night
of Passover continue:

הַיּוֹם יוֹם אֶחָד לָעֹמֶר.

Hayom yom echad la'omer.
This day is first day of the *Omer*.

If your seder is being held on Passover after the first two days,
use the following formulation and fill in the correct day
of the *Omer*, remembering that the first day of the *Omer* is the
second day of Passover.

הַיּוֹם _____ יָמִים לָעֹמֶר.

Hayom _____ yamim la'omer.
Today is the _____ day of the *Omer*.

2-שְׁנֵי 3-שְׁלֹשָׁה 4-אַרְבָּעָה 5-חֲמִשָּׁה 6-שִׁשָּׁה

2-shnei, 3-shlosha, 4-arba'a, 5-chamisha, 6-shisha

READERS

וְלָקַחְתִּי אֶתְכֶם לִי לְעָם וְהָיִיתִי לָכֶם לֵאלֹהִים

V'lakachti etchem li l'am v'hayiti lachem leilohim

"And I will take you to be my people and I will be your God" (EXODUS 6:7).

The fourth cup we drink tonight is linked to the verse from Exodus which tells of God's promise to create a special relationship with Israel. We therefore honor women who, by teaching Jewish texts and promoting Jewish education, have brought individual Jews into a relationship with God and the Jewish people. We dedicate this cup to: Asenath Bat Samuel Barazani, Rachel Morpugo, Rebecca Gratz, Judith Kaplan Eisenstein, and Nechama Leibowitz.

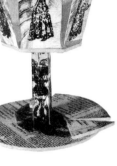

Invite people around the table to add names of women to honor with this cup. Select and read a biography of one of these women from Appendix I. Alternatively, choose a woman from your own family or community and share her story. Lift the cup and recite the blessing.

בְּרוּכָה אַתְּ יָהּ אֱלֹהֵינוּ רוּחַ הָעוֹלָם
בּוֹרֵאת פְּרִי הַגָּפֶן.

B'rucha at yah eloheinu ruach ha'olam
boreit p'ri hagafen.

or

בָּרוּךְ אַתָּה יְיָ אֱלֹהֵינוּ מֶלֶךְ הָעוֹלָם
בּוֹרֵא פְּרִי הַגָּפֶן.

Baruch atah adonai eloheinu melech ha'olam
borei p'ri hagafen.

You are Blessed, Our God, Spirit of the World,
who creates the fruit of the vine.

Drink the fourth cup.

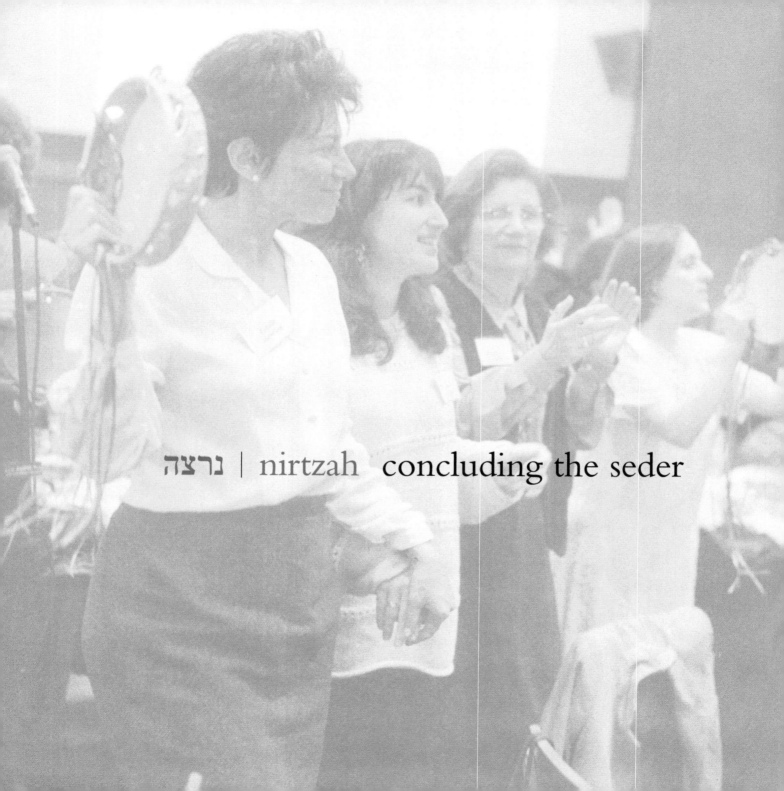

נרצה | nirtzah concluding the seder

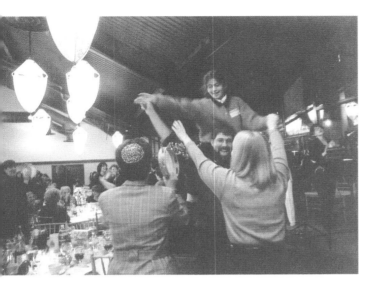

ALL

How does the journey to freedom continue?

READERS

Risking together what we never imagined possible on our own, we keep walking. The sea rises to our nostrils. Then, with a breath, the waters part.

Following fire and cloud, we stumble through endless desert. At night we build fragile shelters that sway in the wind. The water is too bitter to drink. Even manna sometimes tastes like sand.

Some cry out for Egypt, longing to return to the known.

ALL

How does our journey to freedom continue?

READERS

We re-awaken deep yearnings: for history and song, for learning and connection.

We glimpse new possibilities: for our lives and our communities, for our families and our world.

Some begin to plot change immediately. Others sit in the silence and absorb.

ALL

For ours is a holy journey. We falter, but will not turn back. Embracing the challenge of tradition, we clear new paths to the future. Ours is a holy journey, a journey towards new song.

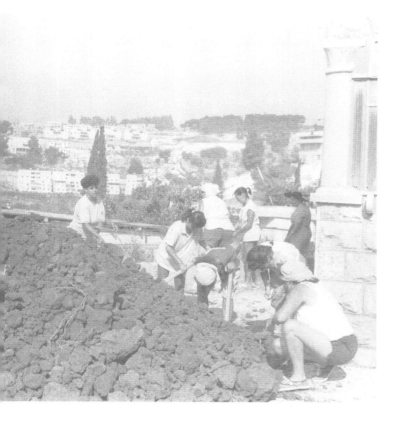

READERS

For hundreds of years, seders have concluded with the words: "Next year in Jerusalem."

Jerusalem. A name that means city of peace, integrity, wholeness.

Jerusalem. A city of walls, ancient and new. Walls of apricot Jerusalem stone. Walls of misunderstanding, hatred, and violence between religious and secular, Jew and Arab, woman and man.

Jerusalem, what is our hope for your rebuilding?

ALL

A year of equality and inclusiveness.

A year of wholeness for our people.

A year of peace for all the peoples who sing to you, Jerusalem.

לשנה הבאה | L'SHANAH HABA'AH

לְשָׁנָה הַבָּאָה בִּירוּשָׁלָיִם

L'shanah haba'a bi'y'rushalayim
Next year in Jerusalem.

> **Do Something!** Make sure your money is being used to empower women! As you consider your *tzedakah* budget for the year, set aside at least 18 percent for projects that specifically support women and girls.

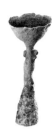

Pass around the Miriam's Cup so everyone can take a sip of water.

תפילת הדרך | T'FILLAT HADERECH

May we be blessed as we go on our way,
May we be guided in peace,
May we be blessed with health and joy,
May this be our blessing, Amen.
May we be sheltered by the wings of peace,
May we be kept in safety and in love,
May grace and compassion find their way to every soul,
May this be our blessing, Amen.
Amen, Amen, may this be our blessing, Amen. (2x)

ברכת המזון B'IRKAT HAMAZON GRACE AFTER MEALS

In this version of the complete *Birkat Hamazon*, we alternate using the feminine and masculine God language.

When there are three or more adults present at the table, they constitute a quorum or *zimun*, with one adult formulaically inviting the others to join in *Birkat Hamazon*. The word *eloheynu* (our God) is added to the *zimun* if ten or more adults are present.

LEADER

חֲבֵרוֹתַי וַחֲבֵרַי נְבָרֵךְ׃

Chaverotay vechaveray nevarech.

GROUP, THEN LEADER

יְהִי שֵׁם יְיָ מְבֹרָךְ מֵעַתָּה וְעַד עוֹלָם.

Yehi shem adonay mevorach me'atah ve'ad olam.

LEADER

בִּרְשׁוּת חֲבֵרוֹתַי וַחֲבֵרַי נְבָרֵךְ
(אֱלֹהֵינוּ) שֶׁאָכַלְנוּ מִשֶּׁלָּה.

Birshut chaverotay vechaveray nevarech
(eloheynu) she'achalnu mishelah.

GROUP, THEN LEADER

בְּרוּכָה (אֱלֹהֵינוּ) שֶׁאָכַלְנוּ
מִשֶּׁלָּה וּבְטוּבָה חָיִּינוּ.

Beruchah (eloheynu) she'achalnu
mishelah uvtuvah chayinu.

ALL

בְּרוּכָה הִיא וּבָרוּךְ שְׁמָהּ.

Beruchah hi uvaruch shemah.

בָּרוּךְ אַתָּה יהוה אֱלֹהֵינוּ מֶלֶךְ הָעוֹלָם
הַזָּן אֶת הָעוֹלָם כֻּלּוֹ בְּטוּבוֹ
בְּחֵן בְּחֶסֶד וּבְרַחֲמִים:
הוּא נוֹתֵן לֶחֶם לְכָל־בָּשָׂר כִּי לְעוֹלָם חַסְדּוֹ:
וּבְטוּבוֹ הַגָּדוֹל תָּמִיד לֹא חָסַר לָנוּ
וְאַל יֶחְסַר־לָנוּ מָזוֹן לְעוֹלָם וָעֶד
בַּעֲבוּר שְׁמוֹ הַגָּדוֹל:
כִּי הוּא אֵל זָן וּמְפַרְנֵס לַכֹּל
וּמֵטִיב לַכֹּל וּמֵכִין מָזוֹן
לְכָל־בְּרִיּוֹתָיו אֲשֶׁר בָּרָא:
בָּרוּךְ אַתָּה יהוה הַזָּן אֶת הַכֹּל:

נוֹדֶה לְךָ יְיָ אֱלֹהֵינוּ
עַל שֶׁהִנְחַלְתָּ לְאִמּוֹתֵינוּ וְלַאֲבוֹתֵינוּ
אֶרֶץ חֶמְדָּה טוֹבָה וּרְחָבָה;
וְעַל שֶׁהוֹצֵאתָנוּ יְיָ אֱלֹהֵינוּ
מֵאֶרֶץ מִצְרָיִם,
וּפְדִיתָנוּ מִבֵּית שְׁפָחוֹת וַעֲבָדִים,
וְעַל בְּרִיתְךָ שֶׁחָתַמְתָּ בְּלִבֵּנוּ,
וְעַל תּוֹרָתְךָ שֶׁלִּמַּדְתָּנוּ,
וְעַל חֻקֶּיךָ שֶׁהוֹדַעְתָּנוּ,
וְעַל חַיִּים, חֵן, וָחֶסֶד שֶׁחוֹנַנְתָּנוּ,
וְעַל אֲכִילַת מָזוֹן שֶׁאַתְּ זָנָה
וּמְפַרְנֶסֶת אוֹתָנוּ תָּמִיד,
בְּכָל יוֹם, וּבְכָל עֵת, וּבְכָל שָׁעָה.

וְעַל־הַכֹּל יהוה אֱלֹהֵינוּ
אֲנַחְנוּ מוֹדִים לָךְ וּמְבָרְכִים אֹתָךְ
יִתְבָּרַךְ שִׁמְךָ בְּפִי כָל־חַי תָּמִיד לְעוֹלָם וָעֶד:
כַּכָּתוּב, וְאָכַלְתָּ וְשָׂבָעְתָּ וּבֵרַכְתָּ אֶת־יהוה

Baruch atah Adonai, eloheinu melech ha-olam,
ha-zan et ha-olam kulo, b'tuvo,
b'chein b'chesed u-v'rachamim.
Hu notein lechem l'chol basar, ki l'olam chasdo.
Uv'tuvo ha-gadol, tamid lo chasar lanu,
v'al yech'sar lanu, mazon l'olam va-ed.
Ba-avur sh'mo ha-gadol
ki hu El zan u-m'farneis la-kol,
u-meitiv la-kol, u-meichin mazon
l'chol bri'otav asher bara.
Baruch atah Adonai, ha-zan et ha-kol.

Nodeh lach Adonai eloheinu,
al she-hinchalt l'imoteinu ve'la-avoteinu
eretz chemda tovah u-r'chavah.
V'al she-hotzeitinu Adonai eloheinu
mei-eretz Mitzrayim,
u-f'ditinu mi-beit shefachot v'avadim,
v'al briteich she-chatamt b'libeinu,
v'al torateich she-limad'tinu,
v'al chukka-ich she-hodatinu,
v'al chayim chein va-chesed she-chonantinu,
v'al achilat mazon she-at zanah
um'farneset otanu tamid,
b'chol yom, uv'chol eit, uv'chol sha'ah.

V'al ha-kol Adonai eloheinu
anachnu modim lach, u-m'varchim otach,
yitbarach shimcha b'fi chol chai tamid l'olam va-ed.
Ka-katuv, v'achalta, v'savata u-veirachta et-Adonai

114

אֱלֹהֶיךָ עַל־הָאָרֶץ הַטּוֹבָה אֲשֶׁר נָתַן־לָךְ:
בָּרוּךְ אַתָּה יהוה עַל־הָאָרֶץ וְעַל־הַמָּזוֹן:

רַחֲמִי יָהּ אֱלֹהֵינוּ עַל יִשְׂרָאֵל עַמֵּךְ,
וְעַל יְרוּשָׁלַיִם עִירֵךְ,
וְעַל צִיּוֹן מִשְׁכַּן כְּבוֹדֵךְ,
וְעַל מַלְכוּת בֵּית דָּוִד מְשִׁיחֵךְ,
וְעַל הַבַּיִת הַגָּדוֹל וְהַקָּדוֹשׁ
שֶׁנִּקְרָא שְׁמֵךְ עָלָיו.

אֱלֹהֵינוּ אִמֵּנוּ רְעֵינוּ זוּנֵנוּ, פַּרְנְסֵינוּ
וְכַלְכְּלֵינוּ וְהַרְוִיחֵנוּ,
וְהַרְוִיחִי לָנוּ, יָהּ אֱלֹהֵינוּ
מְהֵרָה מִכָּל צָרוֹתֵינוּ.

וְנָא, אַל תַּצְרִיכֵינוּ, יָהּ אֱלֹהֵינוּ
לֹא לִידֵי מַתְּנַת בָּשָׂר וָדָם
וְלֹא לִידֵי הַלְוָאָתָם, כִּי אִם לְיָדֵךְ הַמְּלֵאָה
הַפְּתוּחָה, הַקְּדוֹשָׁה וְהָרְחָבָה,
שֶׁלֹּא נֵבוֹשׁ וְלֹא נִכָּלֵם לְעוֹלָם וָעֶד.

[רְצֵה וְהַחֲלִיצֵנוּ יְיָ אֱלֹהֵינוּ
בְּמִצְוֹתֶיךָ וּבְמִצְוַת יוֹם הַשְּׁבִיעִי
הַשַּׁבָּת הַגָּדוֹל וְהַקָּדוֹשׁ הַזֶּה.
כִּי יוֹם גָּדוֹל וְקָדוֹשׁ הוּא לְפָנֶיךָ
לִשְׁבָּת בּוֹ וְלָנוּחַ בּוֹ בְּאַהֲבָה כְּמִצְוַת
רְצוֹנֶךָ. וּבִרְצוֹנְךָ הָנִיחַ לָנוּ
יְיָ אֱלֹהֵינוּ שֶׁלֹּא תְהֵא צָרָה וְיָגוֹן
וַאֲנָחָה בְּיוֹם מְנוּחָתֵנוּ.
וְהַרְאֵנוּ יְיָ אֱלֹהֵינוּ בְּנֶחָמַת צִיּוֹן עִירֶךָ
וּבְבִנְיַן יְרוּשָׁלַיִם עִיר קָדְשֶׁךָ
כִּי אַתָּה הוּא בַּעַל הַיְשׁוּעוֹת וּבַעַל הַנֶּחָמוֹת.]

elohecha, al ha-aretz ha-tovah asher natan lach.
Baruch atah Adonai, al ha-aretz v'al ha mazon.

Rachami Yah eloheinu al Yisrael ameich,
v'al Yeru-shalayim ireich,
v'al Tzion mishkan k'vodeich,
v'al malchut beit David m'shicheich,
v'al ha-bayit ha-gadol v'ha-kadosh
she-nikra sh'meich alav.

Eloheinu imeinu, re'inu zuninu farnesinu
v'chal'kelinu v'harvichinu,
v'harvechi lanu Ya eloheinu
m'heira mikol tzaroteinu.

V'na al tatz'richinu Yah eloheinu,
lo lidei mat'nat basar va-dam,
v'lo lidei halva'atam, ki im l'yadeich ha-m'leyah
ha-p'tuchah ha-k'doshah v'harchavah
she-lo neivosh v'lo nikaleim l'olam va-ed.

On Shabbat add:
[R'tzei v'hachalitzeinu Adonai eloheinu
b'mitzvotecha, u-v'mitzvat yom ha-shvi'i
ha-shabbat ha-gadol v'ha-kadosh ha-zeh,
ki yom zeh gadol v'kadosh hu l'fanecha,
lishbot bo v'lanuach bo b'ahavah k'mitzvat
r'tzonecha. U-virtzoncha haniach lanu
Adonai eloheinu she-lo t'hei tzara v'yagon
v'anacha b'yom m'nuchateinu.
V'hareinu Adonai eloheinu b'nechamat Tzion irecha,
u-b'vinyan Yerushalayim ir kadshecha,
ki atah hu ba'al ha-yeshuot, u-va'al ha-nechamot.]

אֱלֹהֵינוּ וֵאלֹהֵי אֲבוֹתֵינוּ וְאִמּוֹתֵינוּ
יַעֲלֶה וְיָבֹא וְיַגִּיעַ וְיֵרָאֶה וְיֵרָצֶה
וְיִשָּׁמַע וְיִפָּקֵד וְיִזָּכֵר זִכְרוֹנֵנוּ
וּפִקְדוֹנֵנוּ וְזִכְרוֹן אֲבוֹתֵינוּ וְאִמּוֹתֵינוּ
וְזִכְרוֹן יְמוֹת מָשִׁיחַ צִדְקֶךָ וְזִכְרוֹן
יְרוּשָׁלַיִם עִיר קָדְשֶׁךָ וְזִכְרוֹן כָּל עַמְּךָ
בֵּית יִשְׂרָאֵל לְפָנֶיךָ לִפְלֵיטָה וּלְטוֹבָה
לְחֵן וּלְחֶסֶד וּלְרַחֲמִים לְחַיִּים
וּלְשָׁלוֹם בְּיוֹם חַג הַמַּצּוֹת הַזֶּה:
זָכְרֵנוּ יהוה אֱלֹהֵינוּ בּוֹ לְטוֹבָה
וּפָקְדֵנוּ בוֹ לִבְרָכָה וְהוֹשִׁיעֵנוּ בוֹ לְחַיִּים:
וּבִדְבַר יְשׁוּעָה וְרַחֲמִים חוּס וְחָנֵּנוּ
וְרַחֵם עָלֵינוּ וְהוֹשִׁיעֵנוּ כִּי אֵלֶיךָ
עֵינֵינוּ כִּי אֵל מֶלֶךְ חַנּוּן וְרַחוּם אָתָּה:

וּבְנֵה יְרוּשָׁלַיִם עִיר הַקֹּדֶשׁ בִּמְהֵרָה
בְיָמֵינוּ. בְּרוּכָה אַתְּ יָהּ בּוֹנָה
בְרַחֲמֶיהָ יְרוּשָׁלַיִם. אָמֵן.

בָּרוּךְ אַתָּה יְיָ אֱלֹהֵינוּ מְקוֹר הַחַיִּים,
הָאֵל אָבִינוּ מְקוֹרֵנוּ אַדִּירֵנוּ בּוֹרְאֵנוּ גּוֹאֲלֵנוּ
יוֹצְרֵנוּ קְדוֹשֵׁנוּ קְדוֹשׁ יִשְׂרָאֵל, רוֹעֵנוּ
רוֹעֵה יִשְׂרָאֵל הָאֵל הַטּוֹב וְהַמֵּטִיב לַכֹּל
שֶׁבְּכָל יוֹם וָיוֹם הוּא הֵטִיב הוּא מֵטִיב
הוּא יֵיטִיב לָנוּ. הוּא גְּמָלָנוּ הוּא גוֹמְלֵנוּ
הוּא יִגְמְלֵנוּ לָעַד לְחֵן לְחֶסֶד וּלְרַחֲמִים
וּלְרֶוַח הַצָּלָה וְהַצְלָחָה
בְּרָכָה וִישׁוּעָה נֶחָמָה פַרְנָסָה וְכַלְכָּלָה
וְרַחֲמִים וְחַיִּים וְשָׁלוֹם וְכָל טוֹב,
וּמִכָּל טוּב לְעוֹלָם אַל יְחַסְּרֵנוּ.

הָרַחֲמָנָה הִיא תִּשְׁכֹּן אִתָּנוּ לְעוֹלָם וָעֶד.

Eloheinu v'elohey avoteinu v'imoteinu
ya'aleh v'yavo v'yagiah v'yera-eh v'yeratzeh
v'yishama v'yipakeid v'yizacheir zichroneinu
ufikdoneinu v'zichron avoteinu v'imoteinu
v'zichorn yemot mashi-ach tzidkecha v'zichron
yerushalayim ir kodshecha v'zichron kol amcha
beit yisrael lefaneicha lefleita uletovah
lechein ulechesed ulerachamim lechayim
uleshalom beyom chag hamatzot hazeh.
Zochreinu Adonai eloheinu bo letovah
ufakdeynu vo livracha vehoshi'einu vo lechayim.
Uvidvar yeshua verachamim chus vechaneinu
verachem aleinu vehoshi-einu ki eileicha
eineinu ki El melech chanun verachum atah.

Uv'nei yerushalayim ir ha-kodesh bi-m'heira
v'yameinu. Brucha at Yah bonah
verachameiha yerushalayim. Amen.

Baruch atah Adonai, eloheinu mekor ha-chayim:
ha-el, avinu, mekoreinu, adireinu, boreinu, go'aleinu,
yotz'reinu, k'dosheinu, k'dosh yisrael, ro'einu,
ro'ei yisrael, ha-el ha-tov v'ha-meitiv la-kol
she-b'chol yom va-yom hu heitiv, hu meitiv,
hu yeitiv lanu. Hu g'malanu, hu gom'leinu,
hu yig'm'leinu la'ad l'chein l'chesed ul'rachamim
ul'revach hatzala v'hatz'lacha
b'racha viyshua nechama parnasa v'chalkala.
V'rachamim v'chayim v'shalom v'chol tov,
u-mi-kol tuv l'olam al y'chasreinu.

Ha-rachamana hi tishkon itanu l'olam va-ed.

הָרַחֲמָן הוּא יִתְבָּרַךְ בַּשָּׁמַיִם וּבָאָרֶץ.

Ha-rachaman hu yitbarach ba-shamayim u-va-aretz.

הָרַחֲמָנָה הִיא תִּשְׁתַּבַּח לְדוֹר דּוֹרִים וְתִתְפָּאֵר
בָּנוּ לָעַד וּלְנֵצַח נְצָחִים
וְתִתְהַדַּר בָּנוּ לָעַד וּלְעוֹלְמֵי עוֹלָמִים.

Ha-rachamana hi tishtabach l'dor dorim v'titpa'eir
banu la'ad u-l'neitzach n'tzachim,
v'tit'hadar banu la-ad u-l'olmei olamim.

הָרַחֲמָן הוּא יְפַרְנְסֵנוּ בְּכָבוֹד.

Ha-rachaman hu y'farneseinu b'chavod.

הָרַחֲמָנָה הִיא תִּשְׁבּוֹר עָלֵנוּ מֵעַל צַוָּארֵנוּ
וְהִיא תּוֹלִיכֵנוּ קוֹמְמִיּוּת לְאַרְצֵנוּ.

Ha-rachamana hi tishbor uleinu mei-al tzavareinu
v'hi tolicheinu komemiyut l'artzeinu.

הָרַחֲמָן הוּא יִשְׁלַח בְּרָכָה מְרֻבָּה
בַּבַּיִת הַזֶּה וְעַל שֻׁלְחָן זֶה שֶׁאָכַלְנוּ עָלָיו.

Ha-rachaman hu yishlach b'racha m'ruba
ba-bayit ha-zeh, v'al shulchan zeh she-achalnu alav.

הָרַחֲמָנָה הִיא תִּשְׁלַח לָנוּ אֶת אֵלִיָּהוּ הַנָּבִיא
זָכוּר לַטּוֹב וִיבַשֶּׂר לָנוּ בְּשׂוֹרוֹת טוֹבוֹת
יְשׁוּעוֹת וְנֶחָמוֹת.

Ha-rachamana hi tishlach lanu et eliyahu ha-navi
zachur la-tov, vivaser lanu b'sorot tovot
y'shuot v'nechamot.

הָרַחֲמָן הוּא יְבָרֵךְ אֶת כָּל הַמְּסוּבִּין
וְהַמְּסוּבּוֹת כָּאן.

Ha-rachaman hu y'vareich et kol ha-m'subim
ve-ham'subot kan.

הָרַחֲמָנָה הִיא תְּבָרֵךְ אוֹתָנוּ וְאֶת כָּל אֲשֶׁר לָנוּ,
כְּמוֹ שֶׁנִּתְבָּרְכוּ אִמּוֹתֵינוּ שָׂרָה,
רִבְקָה, לֵאָה וְרָחֵל הֵיטִיב טוֹבַת טוֹב טוֹב,
וַאֲבוֹתֵינוּ אַבְרָהָם, יִצְחָק וְיַעֲקֹב
בַּכֹּל מִכֹּל כֹּל, כֵּן תְּבָרֵךְ אוֹתָנוּ כֻּלָּנוּ
יַחַד בִּבְרָכָה שְׁלֵמָה, וְנֹאמַר אָמֵן.

Harachamana hi tevareich otanu v'et kol asher lanu,
k'mo she-nit'barchu imoteinu sarah,
rivkah, le-ah, ve-rachel heytiv tovat tov tov,
va-avoteinu avraham, yitzchak v'ya'akov,
ba-kol mi-kol kol, kein tevareich otanu kulanu
yachad bi-vracha sh'leima v'nomar amen.

בַּמָּרוֹם יְלַמְּדוּ עֲלֵיהֶן וְעָלֵינוּ
זְכוּת שֶׁתְּהֵא לְמִשְׁמֶרֶת שָׁלוֹם.
וְנִשָּׂא בְרָכָה מֵאֵת יְיָ
וּצְדָקָה מֵאֱלֹהֵי יִשְׁעֵנוּ. וְנִמְצָא חֵן
וְשֵׂכֶל טוֹב בְּעֵינֵי אֱלֹהִים וְאָדָם.

Bamarom yelamdu aleihen v'aleinu
z'chut she-t'hei l'mishmeret shalom.
V'nisa v'racha mei-eit Adonai,
u-tz'daka mei-elohei yish'einu v'nimtza chein
v'seichel tov b'einei elohim v'adam.

הָרַחֲמָנָה הִיא תַּנְחִילֵנוּ יוֹם שֶׁכֻּלוֹ]
שַׁבָּת וּמְנוּחָה לְחַיֵּי הָעוֹלָמִים.[

הָרַחֲמָנָה הִיא תַּנְחִילֵנוּ יוֹם שֶׁכֻּלוֹ טוֹב.

הָרַחֲמָן הוּא יְבָרֵךְ אֶת מְדִינַת יִשְׂרָאֵל
וִירוּשָׁלַיִם עִיר הַקֹּדֶשׁ וִיבִיאֵם לִגְאֻלָּה שְׁלֵמָה.

הָרַחֲמָנָה הִיא תִּתֵּן אַחֲוָה בֵּין בְּנֵי
וּבְנוֹת שָׂרָה וּבֵין בְּנֵי וּבְנוֹת הָגָר.

הָרַחֲמָן הוּא יְבָרֵךְ אֶת כָּל אַחֵינוּ
וַאֲחַיוֹתֵינוּ הַנְּתוּנִים בְּצָרָה,
וְתוֹצִיאָן מֵאֲפֵלָה לְאוֹרָה.

הָרַחֲמָנָה הִיא תְּזַכֵּנוּ לִימוֹת הַמָּשִׁיחָה
וּלְחַיֵּי הָעוֹלָם הַבָּא.

מִגְדוֹל יְשׁוּעוֹת עוֹלָמוֹ וְעֹשֶׂה חֶסֶד
לִמְשִׁיחוֹ וְתוֹצִיא כְאוֹר צִדְקָתוֹ עַד עוֹלָם.
עֹשֶׂה שָׁלוֹם בִּמְרוֹמָיו הוּא יַעֲשֶׂה שָׁלוֹם עָלֵינוּ
וְעַל כָּל יוֹשְׁבוֹת תֵּבֵל, וְאִמְרוּ אָמֵן.

יְראוּ אֶת יָהּ קְדֹשֶׁיהָ כִּי אֵין מַחְסוֹר לִירֵאֶיהָ.
כְּפִירִים רָשׁוּ וְרָעֵבוּ וְדֹרְשׁוֹת יָהּ לֹא תַחְסַרְנָה
כָּל טוֹב. הוֹדוּ לְיָהּ כִּי טוֹבָה כִּי לְעוֹלָם חַסְדָּהּ.
פּוֹתַחַת אֶת יָדֵךְ וּמַשְׂבִּיעָה לְכָל חַי רָצוֹן.
בְּרוּכָה הָאִשָּׁה אֲשֶׁר תִּבְטַח בְּיָהּ וְהָיְתָה יָהּ
מִבְטָחָהּ. נַעֲרָה הָיִיתִי גַּם זָקַנְתִּי וְלֹא רָאִיתִי
צַדִּיקִים עוֹזְבִים מְבַקְשֵׁי לָחֶם.
יָהּ עֹז לְעַמָּהּ תִּתֵּן יָהּ תְּבָרֵךְ אֶת עַמָּהּ בַשָּׁלוֹם.

On Shabbat add:

[Harachamana hi tanchileinu yom she-kulo
Shabbat u-m'nucha l'chayei ha-olamim.]

Harchamana hi tanchileinu yom shekulo tov.

Harachaman hu yevareich et medinat yisrael
v'yerushalyim ir hakodesh vi'vi-em lig'ula shleimah.

Harachamana hi titein achava beyn benay
uvnot sarah uveyn benay uvnot hagar.

Harachaman hu yevareich et kol acheynu
v'achyoteinu han'tunim b'tzarah
v'totzi-en mei-afeila l'orah.

Harachamana hi t'zakeinu limot ham'shicha
ul'chayei ha-olam ha-ba.

Migdol y'shuot olamo v'oseh chesed
lim'shicho v'totzi ch'or tzidkato ad olam.
Oseh shalom bimromav, hu ya'aseh shalom aleinu
v'al kol Yisrael, v'al kol yoshvot teiveil v'imru amen.

Y'ru et Yah k'dosheiha, ki ein machsor lirei-eiha.
K'firim rashu v'ra-eivu, v'dorshot Yah lo tachsarna
kol tov. Hodu le-Yah ki tovah, ki l'olam chasdah.
Potachat et yadeich u-masbia-ah l'chol chai ratzon.
Brucha ha-ishah asher tivtach ve-Yah, v'hayta Yah
mivtachah. Na-arah hayiti gam zakanti, v'lo rayiti
tzadikim ozvim m'vak-shey lachem.
Yah oz l'amah titein, Yah tevareich et amah va-shalom.

Leader: Friends, let us give thanks!

Group, then leader: May the name of The Beneficent be praised now and always.

Leader: May the name of The Incomparable be praised now and always.

With your consent: We praise (our God) the one whose food we have eaten.

All: Praised is (our God) the one whose food we have eaten, and by whose goodness we live.

Leader: Praised is (our God) the one whose food we have eaten, and by whose goodness we live.

All: Praised be God and praised be God's name.

Praise is yours, Righteous One our God, Ruler of all, who every day invites the world to a feast of goodness, compassion and love. You feed us; you sustain us. You overwhelm us with your goodness. You provide for all. You love endlessly. Because you are so good to us, we never lacked sustenance in the past. And we hope that we will never lack food in the future. This you do for your own renown that we may know you as the one who sustains and supports all and prepares the food each creature needs. Blessed are you, Provider, who sustains all.

So we thank you Bountiful One our God: Because you granted our ancestors a land desirable, good and wide. And you extricated us,

Compassionate One our God, from the straits of Egypt. You freed us from being at home in servitude. And for the promise you sealed within our hearts. And for your Torah-teaching which you impart to us. And for the limits of conduct which you made us know. And for life, for beauty, for love, with which you are so generous. And for the joy of eating which you allow us, all the while nourishing us every day, every moment.

For all this Incomparable our God we thankfully confess and worship you, whose name is praised by ever-new expressions of life. We do this as Torah states: "Eat your fill praising The Gracious One your God for the earthly goodness which God freely gave you." Therefore we say: "Blessed are you Beneficent One for the land and the food."

Be loving Compassionate One our God to Israel your folk, Jerusalem your city, and Zion your glory's shrine. Remember David's throne and the holy house, the Temple of grandeur where it was so easy to call on you. God, parent, provider, sustainer, you nourish and support and still keep us independent. Kind One our God, keep us free from needs that enslave us. Permit us not to depend on human handouts or loans. But may we depend on your full, yet broadly open hand. Always spare us shame and disgrace.

On Shabbat:

[In commanding us Mighty One our God, you impart to us the strength to fulfill the mitzvah. We thank you for the mitzvah of the seventh day, the

great Shabbat, the Holy Shabbat, this Shabbat. A great and holy day it is. It is a day in which we live in your presence. We rest in it, we relax in it, loving you all the more for the limits you have set on our actions by your will. On this day of rest, Reviver our God, may there be no pain, no worry, no oppression, no anxiety and no sighing. On this Shabbat day Bright One our God, open our eyes to the vision of the consolation of Zion and the upbuilding of Jerusalem. For you are at liberty to freely give salvation and consolation.]

Our God, our ancients' God, may our prayers rise and come to you, and be beheld, and be acceptable. Let it be heard, acted upon, remembered – the memory of us and all our needs, the memory of our ancestors, the memory of messianic days, the memory of Jerusalem your holy city, and the memory of all your kin, the house of Israel, all surviving in your presence. Act for goodness and grace, love and care; for life, well-being and peace, on this festival of matzot.

Remember us this day, All-Knowing our God, for goodness. Favor us this day with blessing. Redeem us this day for life. With your redeeming and nurturing word, be kind and generous. Act tenderly on our behalf, and grant us victory over all our trials. Truly, our eyes turn toward you, for you are a providing God; gracious and merciful are you.

Make this world a place of holiness, now in our own lifetime as you rebuild Jerusalem.

Blessed are you, Compassionate One, who in building up mercy builds Jerusalem. Amen!

Blessed are you The Beneficent One our God, sovereign though hidden. Day by day you do good according to that day's needs. So you did act out of your goodness, and so you will deal well with us in the future. You give of your self, You gave of your self, You will give of your self, freely to us, completely and kindly mercifully and abundantly, to save us, to prosper us, to bless us, to redeem us, to console us, to sustain and support us, in mercy, life and goodness, while not diminishing the good you hold in store for us for eternity.

Compassionate One, dwell with us forever.

Caring One, be involved in our heaven and in our earth.

Loving One, praised by each generation to the next, take pride in us always. May our lives honor you in this world and in the next.

Merciful One, let us earn in an honorable way. Liberating One, break the restraints that make us strangers. Lead us home with dignity.

Generous One, send abundant blessedness to this home and to this table.

God of pleasant surprises — how blessed it is to remember Elijah the prophet — send to us soon the good news of redemption and consolation.

Compassionate One! Bless all who are dining here.

Compassionate One! Bless us and all that is ours. As You blessed our mothers Sarah, Rebecca, Rachel and Leah, with all goodness, and as You blessed our fathers Abraham, Isaac and Jacob with wholeness, thus bless us with a perfect blessing. And let us say, Amen.

Sublime One, interpret our deeds as flowing from good intentions, worthy of blessing from you. Helping God, accept our act of thanksgiving as a favor on your part. May we be found pleasant and wise by you and by our comrades.

On Shabbat:

[Compassionate One! Anchor us and settle us, so that our true home be established in time that is altogether Shabbat, in space that is altogether tranquil, and in life that is altogether alive.]

Compassionate One! Make a day altogether good!

Compassionate One! Bless the State of Israel with Jerusalem its holy city. Bring full redemtion to them both.

Compassionate One! Create a caring bond between the children of Sarah and the children of Hagar.

Compassionate One! Send redemption to all our sisters and brothers who suffer distress and oppression, and bring them from darkness to light.

Compassionate One! Enable us to move toward messianic days, toward a perfected world. May your sovereignty shine in the world. Help us to live so that we be worthy of the messianic days and the coming world. God! We know that you make peace on high. Grant peace to us and to all Israel. Jews live in many lands, among many nations who also need peace. Grant us peace.

Revere Yah, you who make God holy! Revering only God, what will you lack? Those who are self-sufficient like young lions may starve in relying on their own strength. But those who seek only The Source — they will not miss all that is good. Thank The Radiance who is so good, whose kindness is ever in the world, whose will it is for hands to open and satisfy all who live. Blessed are they who trust in Harmony — The Compassionate will be their trust. I have been young and now I am old, yet never have I seen the righteous abandon those who lack bread. The Mighty One will surely give strength to this folk. The Righteous One will bless this folk with shalom.

ALTERNATIVE VERSION OF ADIR HU: ORAH HI

This song, "Orah Hi," patterns itself after the traditional Passover song "Adir Hu," which is an acrostic poem listing God's many qualities of power, righteousness, oneness, sovereignty, and kindness. "Adir Hu" means "He is mighty." The traditional song speaks of God in masculine terms, celebrating God's power as part of the telling of the story of Passover, and praying for the rebuilding of the Temple.

This alternative version is written in the feminine. Like "Adir Hu," it is a Hebrew acrostic, and it can be sung to the traditional melody. Almost all of its images come from the Bible, from rabbinic literature, and from Jewish mysticism. Yet this song does not dwell on God's power and distance. Rather, it emphasizes God's sharing in human joys and griefs, and God's ability to renew life. These are traits which many modern Jewish women have chosen to ascribe to the Divine as they seek their own ways of understanding God. In this version, we can imagine God's house as the Temple, or as our entire world infused with the *Shekhinah*, the indwelling Presence.

She is light, she is light. May She build her house speedily and in our days. God, build Your house soon — close to us in time and space.

She is wisdom, She is joy, She is tears. May She build her house speedily and in our days. God, build Your house soon — close to us in time and space.

She is splendor, She is a rose, She is a flowing stream. May She build her house speedily and in our days. God, build Your house soon — close to us in time and space.

She is renewal, She is the center, She is oneness. May She build her house speedily and in our days. God, build Your house soon — close to us in time and space.

She is the full moon, She is birth, She is the fountain-source. May She build her house speedily and in our days. God, build Your house soon — close to us in time and space.

She is comfort, She is forgiveness, She is strength. May She build her house speedily and in our days. God, build Your house soon — close to us in time and space.

She is redemption, She is righteousness, She is holiness. May She build her house speedily and in our days. God, build Your house soon — close to us in time and space.

She is a beloved companion, She is a teacher of change, She is complete and perfect. May She build her house speedily and in our days. God, build Your house soon — close to us in time and space.

אוֹרָה הִיא, אוֹרָה הִיא, תִּבְנֶה בֵיתָהּ בְּקָרוֹב
בִּמְהֵרָה, בִּמְהֵרָה, בְּיָמֵינוּ בְּקָרוֹב
אֵלָה בְּנִי, אֵלָה בְּנִי, בְּנִי בֵיתֵךְ בְּקָרוֹב.

Orah hi, orah hi, tivnei veitah bekarov,
bimheira, bimheira, beyameinu bekarov,
elah b'ni, elah b'ni, b'ni veiteich bekarov.

בִּינָה הִיא, גִּילָה הִיא, דִּמְעָה הִיא, תִּבְנֶה בֵיתָהּ בְּקָרוֹב
בִּמְהֵרָה, בִּמְהֵרָה, בְּיָמֵינוּ בְּקָרוֹב
אֵלָה בְּנִי, אֵלָה בְּנִי, בְּנִי בֵיתֵךְ בְּקָרוֹב.

Binah hi, gilah hi, dimah hi, tivnei veitah bekarov,
bimheira, bimheira, beyameinu bekarov,
elah b'ni, elah b'ni, b'ni veiteich bekarov.

הַדַר הִיא, וֶרֶד הִיא, זֶרֶם הִיא, תִּבְנֶה בֵיתָהּ בְּקָרוֹב
בִּמְהֵרָה, בִּמְהֵרָה, בְּיָמֵינוּ בְּקָרוֹב
אֵלָה בְּנִי, אֵלָה בְּנִי, בְּנִי בֵיתֵךְ בְּקָרוֹב.

Hadar hi, vered hi, zerem hi, tivnei veitah bekarov,
bimheira, bimheira, beyameinu bekarov,
elah b'ni, b'ni veiteich bekarov.

חִדּוּשׁ הִיא, טַבּוּר הִיא, יִחוּד הִיא, תִּבְנֶה בֵיתָהּ בְּקָרוֹב
בִּמְהֵרָה, בִּמְהֵרָה, בְּיָמֵינוּ בְּקָרוֹב
אֵלָה בְּנִי, אֵלָה בְּנִי, בְּנִי בֵיתֵךְ בְּקָרוֹב.

Chiddush hi, tibur hi, yichud hi, tivnei veitah bekarov,
bimheira, bimheira, beyameinu bekarov,
elah b'ni, elah b'ni, b'ni veiteich bekarov.

כֵּסֵא הִיא, לֵידָה הִיא, מַעְיָן הִיא, תִּבְנֶה בֵיתָהּ בְּקָרוֹב
בִּמְהֵרָה, בִּמְהֵרָה, בְּיָמֵינוּ בְּקָרוֹב
אֵלָה בְּנִי, אֵלָה בְּנִי, בְּנִי בֵיתֵךְ בְּקָרוֹב.

Keseh hi, leidah hi, ma'yan hi, tivnei veitah bekarov,
bimheira, bimheira, beyameinu bekarov,
elah b'ni, elah b'ni, b'ni veiteich bekarov.

נֶחָמָה הִיא, סְלִיחָה הִיא, עָצְמָה הִיא, תִּבְנֶה בֵיתָהּ בְּקָרוֹב
בִּמְהֵרָה, בִּמְהֵרָה, בְּיָמֵינוּ בְּקָרוֹב
אֵלָה בְּנִי, אֵלָה בְּנִי, בְּנִי בֵיתֵךְ בְּקָרוֹב.

Nechamah hi, selichah hi, otzmah hi, tivnei veitah bekarov,
bimheira, bimheira, beyameinu bekarov,
elah b'ni, elah b'ni, b'ni veiteich bekarov.

פִּדְיוֹן הִיא, צֶדֶק הִיא, קֹדֶשׁ הִיא, תִּבְנֶה בֵיתָהּ בְּקָרוֹב
בִּמְהֵרָה, בִּמְהֵרָה, בְּיָמֵינוּ בְּקָרוֹב
אֵלָה בְּנִי, אֵלָה בְּנִי, בְּנִי בֵיתֵךְ בְּקָרוֹב.

Pidyon hi, tzedek hi, kodesh hi, tivnei veitah bekarov,
bimheira, bimheira, beyameinu bekarov, elah b'ni,
elah b'ni, b'ni veiteich bekarov.

רַעְיָה הִיא, שׁוֹנָה הִיא, תָּמָה הִיא, תִּבְנֶה בֵיתָהּ בְּקָרוֹב
בִּמְהֵרָה, בִּמְהֵרָה, בְּיָמֵינוּ בְּקָרוֹב
אֵלָה בְּנִי, אֵלָה בְּנִי, בְּנִי בֵיתֵךְ בְּקָרוֹב.

Ra'ya hi, shonah hi, tamah hi, tivnei veitah bekarov,
bimheira, bimheira, beyameinu bekarov,
elah b'ni, elah b'ni, b'ni veiteich bekarov.

Appendix II: Biographies for Four Cups

Each year that you use this Haggadah you can substitute different historical figures for the Four Cups. In this way you will be continually adding to your familiarity with women in Jewish history. The following biographical sketches, listed in alphabetical order, are taken from earlier editions of the Ma'yan Haggadah.

Bella Abzug (1920–1998)

We raise this cup to honor Bella Abzug, the first Jewish woman to be elected to the United States Congress on a peace and women's rights platform, a founding Second Wave feminist and a fighter for justice until her last breath. Fiercely committed to *tikkun olam*, Abzug participated in some of the first women's seders, lending her humor, passion and *chutzpah* to the development of this ritual.

Born a month before American women won the right to vote, Bella Savitzky Abzug grew up in the Bronx, where as a young Zionist activist, she raised money by giving impassioned speeches at subway stops. After her father's death, thirteen year-old Abzug challenged her traditional synagogue by reciting *Kaddish* daily. A graduate of Hunter College and Columbia Law School, Abzug defended victims of racial and ideological discrimination. In the 1960s she helped found Women Strike for Peace which protested war and nuclear proliferation. At the age of 50, running with the slogan "A Woman's Place is in the House," Abzug became the first Jewish woman elected to the House of Representatives on a women's rights and civil rights platform. She served three terms in Congress, introducing and writing important legislation on behalf of women, civil liberties and gays and lesbians. Abzug eventually brought her energy and principles to the world stage, founding the Women's Environment and Development Organization (WEDO) to help transform the United Nation's agenda on women, human rights, and the environment. Inspiring generations of young women activists, Bella Abzug showed the world that a Jewish woman who speaks her mind and fights the fight really can make a difference.

See www.jwa.org for more on Bella Abzug, including photos and an extensive bibliography.

Rachel Auerbach (1903–1976)

We raise this cup to honor Rachel Auerbach. A graduate in philosophy from Lwow University in Poland, Rachel Auerbach was a Zionist and a literary modernist. She was also one of the very few Jewish women before World War II to cross the gender barrier to acknowledged and respected artistic expression. When the war broke out in Poland, Auerbach was trapped in the Warsaw Ghetto. She devoted herself to writing stories and essays for the *Oneg Shabbos* project and helped to create a secret ghetto archive, parts of which were retrieved after the war. She also lectured for the ghetto's "popular university," and directed a soup kitchen on Kovno Street, where she tried to keep as many Jews as possible from starving to death. After the ghetto was destroyed, Auerbach continued to write from a hiding place on the Aryan side. When the war ended, she immigrated to Israel where she helped found *Yad Vashem*, Israel's Holocaust Memorial. She organized the Department for Collecting Witness Accounts and continued to chronicle life in Warsaw before the war. She died in Israel in 1976.

Roskies, David. *Literature of Destruction*. Philadelphia: Jewish Publication Society, 1992.

Asenath bat Samuel Barazani (1590–1670)

With this cup we honor Asenath bat Samuel Barazani, a remarkable Kurdistani Jewish woman. Born in 1590 into a family of scholars, Asenath was educated to study and teach Torah. When she married, her *ketubah* included an unheard of stipulation exempting her from housework so that she could devote herself to study. When Asenath's husband died, she assumed his position as the head of the academy that her father Samuel had established, and she became the primary teacher, preacher, interpreter of Jewish law, and fund-raiser for the seminary in Mosul. Her correspondence, written in a precise hand in elegant Hebrew, reveals poetic ability, scholarship, and a clear sense of the urgency of her mission. A traditional woman throughout her life, she trained her son Samuel to carry on the legacy of his grandfather and father, and he became a rabbi and teacher in Baghdad. Asenath's legacy is one of rare honor. A letter to her in 1664 declared, "My lady, my mother, my rabbinate... We are always ready to revere you and serve you truly and faithfully, but please do not forget [to mention] us in your prayers, for surely your prayer is more accepted [by God] and is equal to peace offerings, ascending to high heaven and binding the upper worlds with the earthly one."

Henry, S. and Taitz, E. *Written Out of History: Our Jewish Foremothers*. Fresh Meadows: Biblio Press, 1983; Sabar, Yona. *The Folk Literature of the Kurdistani Jews: An Anthology*. New Haven: Yale University Press, 1982.

Judith Kaplan Eisenstein (1910–1996)

With this cup we honor the memory of Judith Kaplan Eisenstein. In 1922, when Judith Kaplan was twelve years old she made history when she was called to the Torah as the first Bat Mitzvah by her father, Rabbi Mordecai Kaplan (founder of the Reconstructionist movement). This early experience served her well when, after earning bachelor's and master's degrees in music at Columbia University, she became one of the earliest women to teach at the Jewish Theological Seminary. Her book of children's music, *Gateway to Jewish Song*, and her *Heritage of Jewish Music* quickly became classics. In 1934 she married her father's closest disciple, Rabbi Ira Eisenstein, who collaborated with her on some of the seven Jewish cantatas that she wrote during her career. While in her 50s, after raising her family, she earned a doctorate in Sacred Music at Hebrew Union College-Jewish Institute of Religion. She continued teaching rabbis and teachers at Hebrew Union College as well as at the Reconstructionist Rabbinical College, which her husband founded in 1968. Kaplan Eisenstein's life's work reflected her belief that the rich legacy of Jewish music opens the way to the Jewish soul and to a deeper understanding of Jewish history.

Debra Nussbaum Cohen, "The First Bat Mitzvah Dies at the age of 86," Daily News Bulletin of the *Jewish Telegraphic Agency*, February 16, 1996.

Glikl of Hameln (1646–1724)

With this cup we honor Glikl bas Judah Leib and Beila, more commonly known as Glückel of Hameln. Born in 1646 in the German town of Hamburg, Glikl's brief childhood was marked by dislocation due to the expulsion of Jews from her birthplace. By the age of twelve she was betrothed to Haim of Hameln, a young man she had never met but would grow to love deeply over thirty years of marriage. Glikl became a partner in all aspects of Haim's affairs, making business decisions, overseeing finances, and drawing up contracts. As their business grew, so did their family. Glikl survived fourteen pregnancies and raised twelve children to adulthood. A tragic accident in 1689 killed Haim, taking from Glikl "the crown of [her] life." Laden with grief, financial burdens and a challenge to her faith in God, she assumed full responsibility for the family enterprise, travelling to business fairs throughout Western Europe, opening her own stocking factory and store, and skillfully arranging her children's marriages. She also began a project that would claim her a role in history: she began to write her memoirs. Glikl's memoirs invite the reader into the heart and mind of a seventeenth century Jewish woman. Her stories and descriptions of everyday life reflect a keen intelligence and devout piety while providing a window on the spiritual and material reality of Jewish life in pre-modern Europe. We bless this cup of wine in memory of Glikl. We celebrate the vision, creativity and confidence which led her to write, making visible a part of Jewish experience which otherwise would have been forgotten.

Lowenthal, Marvin, trans. *The Memoirs of Gluckel of Hameln*. New York: Schocken Books, 1989.

Rebecca Gratz (1781–1869)

This cup is dedicated to the memory of Rebecca Gratz. Born in Philadelphia on March 4, 1781, Gratz grew up in a large and loving family that always remained central in her life. An observant Jew who lived in the largely Christian elite society of nineteenth century Philadelphia, Gratz was a proud defender of Judaism. Her friendships with non-Jews gave her a forum for developing and expressing her ideas about the importance of religious tolerance in American society. Protective of poor Jews who were vulnerable to proselytizers, she joined women from her community to found the Female Hebrew Benevolent Society which provided food, fuel, shelter, and later an employment bureau and traveler's aid service. Gratz believed that women were uniquely responsible for the preservation of Jewish life in America. All the institutions she established were run by women, most notably the Hebrew Sunday School which provided Jewish women with the unprecedented opportunity to educate boys and girls in a religious context. Rebecca Gratz embodied her own statement that with "an unsubdued spirit" one can conquer all of life's difficulties. She forged a path that we continue to follow and honor through our own commitment to Jewish women's education, self-actualization and community.

Ashton, Dianne. *Rebecca Gratz: Women's Judaism in Antebellum America.* Wayne State University Press, 1997. See www.jwa.org for more extensive biography and primary sources.

Rachel Kagan (1888–1982)

With this cup we honor Rachel Kagan, a woman who was dedicated to ensuring the rights and freedom of women in the newly founded State of Israel. Born in Odessa in 1888, Kagan was educated in secular and religious schools. She went on to study mathematics at the Universities of Odessa and Petrograd. In 1919, Kagan and her husband, Dr. Noah Cohen, immigrated to Palestine and settled in Haifa. Kagan was an outspoken member of the Union of Hebrew Women for Equal Rights in Eretz Yisrael, advocating tirelessly for women's suffrage. Kagan was also active in a nascent women's social service organization, working on behalf of needy families. With Hadassah women in the diaspora, she founded the Women's International Zionist Organization (WIZO) and was elected as its first president. In her capacity as president of WIZO, Kagan was one of two women to sign the Israeli Declaration of Independence. Kagan was elected to the first Knesset of the State of Israel as the sole representative of the women's party formed by WIZO and the Union of Hebrew Women for Equal Rights. She was also elected to the fifth Knesset on the Liberal ticket. Until her death, Kagan remained a sharp critic of modern Israel. She warned repeatedly that the country was not paying enough attention to bridging diverse ethnic groups, leveling economic disparities and educating its youth about the vision of their parents. She expressed deep frustration with a political system that prevented women from wielding significant influence.

Yishai, Yael. *Between the Flag and the Banner: Women in Israeli Politics.* Albany: State of University Press, 1997; Feuerstein, Emil. *Women Who Made History: 40 Portraits of Chalutzot in Eretz Israel.* Ministry of Defense, 1989.

Emma Lazarus (1849–1887)

This cup is dedicated to the memory of Emma Lazarus. Lazarus was born in New York City in 1849, the daughter of an Ashkenazi mother and Sephardic father whose families had been in America since colonial times. Comfortable in their American identity, Lazarus' parents gave her a secular education. Thus, as she explained in 1877, while her "interest and sympathies were loyal to [her] race… [her] religious convictions and the circumstances of [her] life" had led her to feel "somewhat apart from [her] people." All this changed when, moved by the plight of Russian Jews in the 1880s, Lazarus, already a published poet of acclaim and a member of the New York cultural elite, began to educate herself as a Jew. She published *Songs of a Semite*, a collection of poetry with Jewish themes. She wrote essays challenging her non-Jewish readers to reject their anti-semitism, while urging her Jewish audiences to join her in taking an active role in aiding immigrants to America and supporting the resettlement of Palestine. She became involved in helping new immigrants to New York and was inspired by her experience at the port in Castle Gardens to write the now celebrated poem "The New Colossus." In this poem, Lazarus gives voice to the Statue of Liberty, personifying her as a Mother of Exiles who proclaims "Give me your tired, your poor/Your huddled masses yearning to breathe free." Emma Lazarus' life was cut short tragically by cancer, but her words remain as a testament to her passionate embrace of and struggle with her multiple identities as a writer, a woman, an American and a Jew.

Diane Lichtenstein, "Emma Lazarus" in Paula Hyman and Deborah Dash Moore, eds. *Jewish Women in America: An Historical Encyclopedia*, NY: Routledge, 1997. See www.jwa.org for more extensive biography and primary sources.

Nehama Leibowitz (1905–1997)

With this cup we celebrate Nehama Leibowitz, a Torah scholar and teacher who helped countless Jews feel excited about their connection to the Jewish people. Leibowitz was born in 1905 in Riga. She earned a doctorate in Bible Studies from the University of Berlin and in 1931, she and her husband immigrated to Palestine. There she began teaching bible at the Mizrachi Women's Teachers' Seminar in Jerusalem. Leibowitz transmitted the value of the Bible in their everyday lives to tens of thousands of students. She gave a weekly lesson over Israel Radio and distributed self-instruction study guides with questions about the weekly portion. Leibowitz's studies and study guides covering the entire Torah have been published and translated into English, French, Spanish and Dutch. In 1957, the year she joined the faculty of Tel Aviv University, Leibowitz was awarded the coveted Israel Prize for her contributions to education. In 1982 she received the Bialik Prize in Literature and Jewish Studies. An unpretentious woman, when she received an honorary doctorate from Bar-Ilan University, she remarked that she was pleased that a *melamed*, a simple teacher, would be so honored. By the time Leibowitz died at the age of 92 on April 12, 1997, her influence and contributions were recognized by rabbis and scholars around the world. We raise our cup in honor of Nehama Leibowitz, a female pioneer, teacher and role model in the study of Torah, and we rededicate ourselves to continued learning.

"Nehama Leibowitz" *Jerusalem Report*, April 14 1997.

Rachel Luzzatto Morpurgo (1790–1871)

We honor Rachel Luzzatto Morpurgo, the first woman to write and publish modern Hebrew poetry. Rachel Luzzatto was born in Trieste, Italy in 1790 into a family of scholars and mystics. She was educated by her uncles who taught her not only Bible, commentaries and philosophy, but also the art of lithography. From an early age, she assisted them in the Luzzatto family printing business. And through her teens, quite unusual for a girl, she studied Talmud and subsequently, mystical texts. She also earned praise as a skillful seamstress, crafting all the clothes for three generations of women in her family. Despite her parents' wishes, Rachel Luzzatto refused many offers of marriage and waited until she was 29 to marry Jacob Morpurgo. The demands of managing a household and four small children made it difficult for her to write, and Jacob strongly disapproved of her scholarly activities. But she was determined to continue composing verses in celebration of family and community milestones, and she wrote late at night and on *Rosh Chodesh*, when women were traditionally exempted from housework. Morpurgo was honored by her contemporaries who sought her literary opinion even though some confessed disbelief when they first discovered the gender of the poet whose rich Hebrew cadences they admired. Even her husband finally acknowledged her achievements with pride. As we bless this cup, we remember Rachel Luzzatto Morpugo, a woman of spirit and skill, whose poetry transcends time, geography and personal circumstance.

Adelman, Howard. "Finding Women's Voices in Italian Jewish Literature" in Judith R. Baskin, ed. *Women of the Word: Jewish Women and Jewish Writing*. Detroit: Wayne State University Press, 1994.

Doña Gracia Nasi (1510–1569)

With this cup we remember "La Señora," "*Ha'Giveret*," Doña Gracia Nasi, who brought the children of Israel out from the burdens of secrecy and fear. Her birth-name was Beatrice de Luna. Born thirteen years after the Inquisition expelled all Jews from Portugal, Beatrice de Luna was raised by a prosperous Jewish family that chose to become Marranos—outwardly Christian, secretly Jews. Yet even as a young married woman, she began using her wealth and contacts to help other Marranos escape persecution. Rescue became her life's work. Although she was a successful businesswoman, Nasi was arrested once and forced to relocate several times until she finally found safe haven under the protection of the Duke of Ferrara in Italy. There she took the name Gracia (the equivalent of her Hebrew name Hannah) and at age 35, began to live openly as a Jew. She expanded both her business and rescue activities and became a renowned patron of Jewish letters. *The Ferrara Bible*, a 1553 translation from Hebrew to Spanish, is dedicated to "the Very Magnificent Lady" whose "merits have always earned her the most sublime place among our people."

Henry, S. and Taitz, E. *Written Out of History: Our Jewish Foremothers*. Fresh Meadows: Biblio Press, 1983.

Pauline M. Newman (1890–1986)

We raise this cup in honor of Pauline M. Newman. Newman was born to religious parents in Kovno, Lithuania sometime around 1890. In 1901, Newman's widowed mother immigrated to America with her children. Nine year-old Newman went to work in a New York City hairbrush factory. Two years later, she began working among other children in the "kindergarten" at the Triangle Shirtwaist Factory. At the age of sixteen Newman planned and led a rent strike involving 10,000 families in lower Manhattan. It was the largest rent strike New York City had seen, and it catalyzed decades of tenant activism that eventually led to the establishment of rent control. Once Newman's talent for organizing became apparent, the International Ladies' Garment Workers' Union hired her. For more than seventy years she worked for the Union as an organizer, labor journalist, health educator, and government liaison. An acerbic woman whose unorthodox tastes ran to cropped hair and tailored tweed jackets, Newman loved the labor movement. She referred to the ILGWU as her "family" and believed that it was, for all its flaws, the best hope for women garment workers. Newman's "family" also embraced a cross-class circle of women reformers that included Eleanor Roosevelt, Rose Schneiderman and Frieda Miller, Newman's partner of fifty-six years. This circle of women shaped the body of laws and government protections that most workers now take for granted.

Orleck, Annelise. *Common Sense and a Little Fire: Women and Working-Class Politics 1900-1965*. Chapel Hill: University of North Carolina Press, 1995.

Bertha Pappenheim (1859–1936)

This cup is dedicated to the memory of Bertha Pappenheim, a woman who worked hard to free herself from personal obstacles and went on to make a significant contribution to the lives of European Jewish women. Raised in a wealthy Orthodox family in mid-19th century Vienna, Bertha Pappenheim was struck with paralysis as a young woman, after nursing her father through a long terminal illness. Under the care of Joseph Breuer, a colleague of Freud's, she devised a "talking cure" for herself, and as "Anna O," sparked the development of psychoanalysis. She then turned her extraordinary energies to the needs of other women. Infuriated by the disenfranchisement of women in the German Jewish community, she founded the *Judischer Frauenbund*, the first Jewish organization to fight for women's civil and religious rights. To give the next generation of Jews greater access to their legacy, she translated the memoirs of one of her own ancestors, Glikl of Hameln. Deeply committed to social service, Pappenheim took as her lifelong cause the plight of homeless Jewish women. She visited brothels in Eastern Europe, Greece and Turkey where Jewish women were forced to work. She consulted with doctors, social workers, and the police. She campaigned strenuously among the male leadership of local Jewish communities, urging them to address the effects of poverty and social dislocation on Jewish women and their children. Issuing a bitter public report in 1904, Pappenheim rose to international prominence for her relief work and vocational education. In 1907, she founded Isenberg, Europe's first Jewish shelter and group home for single mothers and their children and for girls escaping prostitution. She ran this home for 29 years, personally helping thousands of women.

Henry, S. and Taitz, E. *Written Out of History: Our Jewish Foremothers*. Fresh Meadows: Biblio Press, 1983.

Justine Wise Polier (1903–1987)

This cup is dedicated to Justine Wise Polier, a visionary family court judge and committed social activist who, with her own outstretched arms and great judgments, aided countless disadvantaged children in New York City and beyond. Polier was born in 1903 to Rabbi Stephen Wise and Louise Waterman Wise, parents who raised her to embrace her responsibility to social justice as a Jew and an American. Throughout her college and law school years, she became increasingly involved in helping workers unionize. She aided strikers in the Passaic textile mills throughout the 1920s. The first woman ever appointed as judge in the State of New York, Justine Wise Polier was sworn in as a justice of New York's Domestic Relations Court in 1935. She espoused an activist concept of the law and pioneered the establishment of mental health, educational, and other rehabilitative services for troubled children. She also took a leading role in opposing racial and religious discrimination in public and private facilities. As a committed Jewish leader, Polier spoke out against anti-semitism, urging Jews to lead the battle for human rights for all minorities. Together with her husband, Polier shaped the American Jewish Congress' policy on many progressive issues. After she retired from the bench, Polier continued to work on behalf of disadvantaged children through the Wiltwyck Home and School for Boys, the Citizens Committee for Children and the Children's Defense Fund.

Antler, Joyce. *The Journey Home: Jewish Women and the American Century.* Boston: Free Press, 1997. See www.jwa.org for more extensive biography and primary sources.

Rose Schneiderman (1884–1972)

This cup honors Rose Schneiderman, a 4 foot 9 inches tall red-headed union organizer whose powerful speeches and activism inspired countless women and men to envision better lives. Rose Schneiderman arrived in New York City from Poland in 1890 as an eight year-old with her parents and three younger brothers. Five years later, due to her father's death, Schneiderman was forced to quit school to help support her family. Her first job in a department store demanded sixty-four hours a week of work for subsistence wages. It was at her next job as a sewing machine operator that Schneiderman organized the first woman's local of the Jewish socialist union, United Cloth, Hat, Cap and Millinery Workers. For the next forty-five years, as a leader of the Women's Trade Union League, Schneiderman organized strikes, trained young leaders, helped negotiate labor disputes and worked to establish continuing education programs for women workers. She was an extremely popular speaker who travelled throughout the country enlisting support for labor and women's suffrage. She ran for the United Stated Senate in 1920 and was the only woman appointed in Roosevelt's National Recovery Administration in 1933. Her influence, commitment and persistence were crucial in the drafting and passing of key legislation, including: social security, worker's compensation, the elimination of child labor, maternity leave, safety laws, minimum wage and unemployment insurance. As we drink this cup, we draw inspiration from Rose Schneiderman, who once proclaimed "what the working woman wants is the right to live, not simply exist. The worker must have bread, but she must have roses, too."

Orleck, Annelise. *Common Sense and a Little Fire: Women and Working-Class Politics 1900-1965.* Chapel Hill: University of North Carolina Press, 1995.

Manya Wilbushewitch Shochat (1880–1961)

With this cup we honor Manya Wilbushewitch Shochat. Manya Wilbushewitch, daughter of middle-class Russian Jewish parents, was first exposed to revolutionary ideas while working as a carpenter in her brother's factory in Minsk. Imprisoned in 1899 because of her contacts in revolutionary circles, she became convinced that a Jewish workers' movement would lead to an extension of Jewish civil rights. The charismatic, outspoken young woman participated in the founding of the Jewish Independent Labor Party, which collapsed a few years later in the wake of the Kishinev pogrom. Visiting Palestine in 1904, Shochat concluded that only through collective agricultural settlement could a class of Jewish workers emerge, a pre-condition for building a Jewish homeland. She returned to Palestine in 1907 to help establish the country's first ideologically-based cooperative agricultural settlement at Sejera. A year later, with Israel Shochat whom she later married, she helped found *HaShomer*, a network for the training and support of guards for the increasing number of Jewish settlements. When they extended their work to the creation of a Jewish militia, the Shochats were deported by Turkish authorities. Returning to Palestine in 1919, Manya and Israel Shochat devoted their energies to building the infrastructure of a workers' state. In 1930, Manya Shochat was among the founders of the League for Arab-Jewish Friendship. By the end of her life, the worker's settlements she envisioned had been realized in *kibbutzim* and *moshavim* across Israel.

Shazar, Rachel Katznelson, ed. *The Plough Woman: Memoirs of Pioneer Women of Palestine*. New York: Herzl Press, 1975.

Hannah Greenebaum Solomon (1858–1942)

With this cup, we honor Hannah Greenebaum Solomon, the visionary leader who founded the National Council of Jewish Women, the first national Jewish women's organization in the United States. Hannah Greenebaum Solomon was born in 1858 in Chicago. By the time she was chosen to organize the Jewish Women's Congress at the 1893 World's Columbian Exposition in Chicago, Solomon had become a prominent leader in secular women's circles and in the Jewish community. It was at the close of the Jewish Women's Congress that the National Council of Jewish Women (NCJW) was founded with the goal of promoting social justice, Jewish education, and philanthropy. Solomon was unanimously chosen as its first president. In the next decades, Solomon worked through the NCJW to provide women with Jewish education, unprecedented opportunities for leadership and avenues for helping immigrants. Solomon also founded Chicago's Bureau of Personal Service, which along with NCJW, pioneered social service programs before the establishment of a coordinated Jewish philanthropic effort in Chicago. A friend and colleague of Susan B. Anthony and Jane Addams, Solomon was an outspoken advocate for women's suffrage and women's rights worldwide and the founder of a girls' school in Chicago. Solomon was also a proud liberal Jew, the first woman to speak from many pulpits in America. Wife, mother, grandmother, and great-grandmother, Solomon modeled a life in which extensive community involvement coexisted with a deep commitment to family.

Rogow, Faith. *Gone to Another Meeting*. University of Alabama Press, 1993. See www.jwa.org for more extensive biography and primary sources.

Henrietta Szold (1860–1945)

With this cup we celebrate Henrietta Szold, a towering figure in 20th century history. Born into the German Jewish community in Baltimore in 1860, Henrietta Szold spent the first decades of her life under the tutelage of her father, an erudite European rabbi. Under the *nom de plume* Shulamit, she published articles on Jewish life. Profoundly influenced by the Russian Jews who arrived in Baltimore in the 1880s, Szold opened a night school for immigrants and along with her father, joined one of the first Zionist study circles in America. After her father's death, Szold and her mother and sister moved to New York so that she could study at the Jewish Theological Seminary where she was accepted under the condition that she would not pursue a rabbinic diploma. She continued to work as the primary editor for the Jewish Publication Society while editing and translating manuscripts for Seminary faculty. In 1909, when she was close to fifty, she took her first trip to Palestine. On her return she founded Hadassah, a women's Zionist organization dedicated "to healing the body and soul" of the Jewish people. A brilliant organizer and educator, Szold spent the next decades of her life building a comprehensive health care and social welfare system in Palestine. In the final years of her life she directed Youth Aliyah, which helped to save and resettle close to 50,000 Jewish children from Nazi occupied Europe. As we raise this cup in honor of Henrietta Szold, we recall the charge she once gave a group of Hadassah women, "dare to dream–and when you dream, dream big."

Antler, Joyce. *The Journey Home: Jewish Women and the American Century*. Boston: Free Press, 1997.

Lillian D. Wald (1867–1940)

We dedicate this cup to the memory of Lillian D. Wald who, throughout her life, stretched out her arms and heart in the service of creating a more just society for America's underprivileged. Born in Rochester, New York in 1867, Lillian D. Wald might have said that her life truly began twenty six years later, when as a young nurse, she visited a poor family in a crumbling tenement on the Lower East Side. The largely Jewish immigrant population was in dire need of affordable health care and Wald, through pioneering public health nursing, was going to offer it. During the next decades, Wald founded the Visiting Nurse Service of New York and the Henry Street Settlement, institutions that continue to improve the quality of life for residents of New York City today. Championing the causes of nursing, unionism, tenement reform, women's suffrage, child welfare, and antimilitarism, Wald became a major civic figure in local, national and international arenas. Her commitment to the health of individuals at home became increasingly connected to a concern for the health of nations throughout the world. As we bless this cup, we remember the legacy of Lillian Wald, drawing inspiration from this woman who remained throughout her life "consecrated to the saving of human life, the promotion of happiness and the expansion of good will among people."

Marjorie Feld, "Lillian Wald" in Hyman and Moore, eds. *Jewish Women in America: An Historical Encyclopedia*. New York: Routledge, 1997. See www.jwa.org for more extensive biography and primary sources.

Appendix III: Do Something! Resources

American Friends of Jerusalem Open House
PO Box 1851
NY, NY 10185-1851
www.gay.org.il/joh
joh@gay.org.il

The Jerusalem Open House (JOH) is a grassroots initiative of gay activists in Jerusalem to create a gay community center in Jerusalem. Located in the historic capital of the Jewish people, the House is a beacon of tolerance in a city becoming more and more fragmented.

American Jewish World Service
Women's Empowerment Projects
45 W 36th Street
NY, NY 10018
tel. 800. 889. 7146
www.ajws.org / ajws@ajws.org

The Fund supports activists in developing countries to promote broad social change through empowering women to provide for themselves and their families, to resist and organize against gender oppression, to improve their circumstances and to change the communities in which they live.

Association of Rape Crisis Centers in Israel
to contribute: P.E.F. Israel Endowments Funds
317 Madison Ave., Suite 607
NY, NY 10017

The Association of Rape Crisis Centers in Israel works to gain greater rights and services for its victims, reduce the prevalence of sexual assault and ultimately eradicate this crime from the Israeli landscape.

AVODAH: The Jewish Service Corps
116 E 27th Street, 10th Floor
NY, NY 10016
tel. 212. 545. 7759 fax. 212. 686. 1353
www.avodah.net

AVODAH: The Jewish Service Corps is a year long program for young Jews who want to work on America's pressing social problems.

Center for the Prevention of Sexual and Domestic Violence
936 N 34th St. Suite 200
Seattle, WA 98103
tel. 206. 634. 1903 fax. 206. 634. 0115
www.cpsdv.org / cpsdv@cpsdv.org

An interreligious, educational resource center for religious responses to and the prevention of sexual and domestic violence.

Coalition on the Environment and Jewish Life (COEJL)
443 Park Ave. S. 11th Floor
NY, NY 10016
tel. 212. 532. 7436
www.coejl.org / info@coejl.org

COEJL engages Jewish institutions and individuals in bringing the moral passion of Jewish tradition and social action to environmental stewardship.

Economic Empowerment for Women
New Israel Fund
1101 14th Street NW, 6th Floor
Washington, DC 20005
tel. 202. 842. 0900 or 888. 988. 3863
fax. 202. 842. 0991
www.nif.org / info@nif.org

EEW is dedicated to improving the lives of low-income women and their families in Israel by providing life skills and empowerment training, business training; distribution of small loans for micro-enterprises; and ongoing consultation, network building and support.

HEEB: The New Jewish Review
PO Box 20074
Brooklyn, NY 11202
Ohbaby@heebmagazine.com

A new, clearly hip, publication that describes itself as "...an ambitious antitrust investigation into the monopoly on God...a sweaty prize fight between hip hop and sushi in this corner and klezmer and kugel in the other..."

Jews for Racial and Economic Justice (JFREJ)
135 W 29th St. #600
NY, NY 10001
tel. 212. 647. 8966 fax. 212. 647. 7124
www.jfrej.org / info@jfrej.org

A progressive Jewish voice in debates over racial and ethnic tension and economic disparity in New York City, JFREJ activates the Jewish community as a partner in the struggle for justice through educational forums, workshops, grassroots political campaigns, and a radio show.

Jewish FundS for Justice (JFJ)
330 7th Ave., Suite 1401
New York, NY 10001
tel. 212. 213. 2113 fax. 212. 213. 2233
www.jewishjustice.org / info@jewishjustice.org

JFJ is a national publicly supported foundation that acts on the historic commitment of the Jewish people to *tzedakah* and *tikkun olam*, and fights the feminization of poverty. Groups supported by JFJ's Purim Fund are run by and for women. JFJ has merged with The Shefa Fund and supports their TZEDEC Community Investment Program that invests in low-income community development.

Jewish Organizing Initiative
99 Chauncy St., Suite 600
Boston, MA 02111
tel. 617. 350. 9994 fax. 617. 350. 9995
joi@jewishorganizing.org
www.jewishorganizing.org

The Jewish Organizing Initiative provides Jewish young adults one-year paid fellowships in community organizing.

Jewish Orthodox Feminist Alliance (JOFA)
15 E 26th St., Suite 915
NY, NY 10010
tel. 212. 679. 8500 / 888. 550. JOFA
fax. 212. 679. 7428
www.jofa.org / jofa@jofa.org

JOFA advocates for meaningful participation and equality for women in family, synagogues, houses of learning, and Jewish communal organizations to the full extent possible within *halachah*. JOFA has developed a gender sensitive curriculum that is being used in Orthodox day schools.

Jewish Women's Archive
138 Harvard Street
Brookline, MA 02446
tel. 617. 232. 2258 fax. 617. 975. 0109
www.jwa.org / webmaster@jwa.org

The Jewish Women's Archive records, chronicles, and transmits the rich history of American Jewish women. Their curriculum, *Making Our Wilderness Bloom: Women Who Made American Jewish History*, is being used by middle and high school students as well as by educators across the country for learners of all ages.

Keshet
284 Armory St.
Building G, 2nd floor
Jamaica Plain, MA 02130

Keshet seeks to create a fully welcoming and inclusive Jewish community for gay, lesbian, bisexual, and transgender (GLBT) Jews in Greater Boston. Keshet develops leadership for change among GLBT Jews and allies to effect concrete changes in Jewish institutions' policies and cultures.

Lilith Magazine
250 W 57th St. Suite 2432
NY, NY 10107
tel. 212. 757. 5705
info@lilith.org
www.lilith.org

The award-winning independent Jewish women's magazine which changes the ways Jewish women see themselves and their roles in the Jewish community.

Mavoi Satum
(also funded through New Israel Fund, see above.)
noga@mavoisatum.org or agunot@netvision.net.il
to contribute: P.E.F. Israel Endowments Funds
317 Madison Ave., Suite 607
New York, NY 10017
recommendation for "The Dead End"

Mavoi Satum is a young Israeli organization that empowers *agunot* and advocates on their behalf for changes in the application of Jewish law both in religious divorce and in Israeli civil divorce.

Mazon: A Jewish Response to Hunger
1990 So. Bundy Drive, Suite 260
Los Angeles, CA 90025-5232
tel. 310. 442. 0020 fax. 310. 442. 0030
mazonmail@aol.com
www.mazon.org

MAZON ("food" in Hebrew) raises funds principally from Jews nationwide who donate 3% of the cost of weddings, bar and bat mitzvahs and other joyous events. MAZON provides cash grants to a broad spectrum of nonprofit organizations working to confront hunger.

Moving Traditions
580 Virginia Drive, Suite 141
Fort Washington, PA 19034
tel. 215. 643. 4511
info@movingtraditions.org
www.movingtraditions.org
www.roshhodesh.org

Moving Traditions is an educational organization founded in the belief that women and men are full and equal participants in Judaism. *Rosh Chodesh: It's a Girl Thing*, a program of Moving Traditions, is a values-based, experiential and transdenominational program for pre-teen and teenage girls in grades 6-12 that strengthens self-esteem and Jewish identity, and operates in JCCs, synagogues and day school across North America.

Nashim
Project MUSE
2715 North Charles St.
Baltimore, MD 21218-4319
tel. 410. 516. 6989 fax. 410. 516. 6968
www.muse.jhu.edu / muse@muse.jhu.edu

Nashim: A Journal of Jewish Women's Studies & Gender Issues provides an international, interdisciplinary academic forum for the innovative work being done in the many areas of research that comprise the field of Jewish women's and gender studies.

Project Kesher
2144 Ashland Ave, Suite 3
Evanston, IL 60201
tel. 847. 332. 1994 fax. 847. 332. 2134
projectkesher@projectkesher.org
www.projectkesher.org

Project Kesher develops Jewish women's identity, leadership, community organizing skills and provides economic opportunity in the former Soviet Union, through a grassroots women's movement of 165 groups across eight time zones.

Seeking Common Ground
POB 101958
Denver, CO 80250
tel. 303. 691. 2393
www.s-c-g.org / info@s-c-g.org

SCG is a peace and leadership development program for teens. SCG's Building Bridges for Peace brings together Palestinian, Israeli and American high school women for a summer experience modeled on a feminist perspective of peace building.

YEDID
yedid@yedid.org.il www.yedid.org.il
to contribute: American Supporters of YEDID
301 East 69th St., 17 F
New York, NY 10021
tel 212. 452. 0107

YEDID: The Association for Community Empowerment promotes social justice in Israel by operating Citizen Rights Centers in poor communities throughout the country that work to help individuals and communities to break the cycle of poverty through community empowerment programming, leadership development and grassroots advocacy.

Glossary

Achyoteinu our sisters

Agunot Jewish women whose husbands have refused to give them a *get*, a Jewish bill of divorce

Ashkenazi pertaining to Jews of Central and Eastern European background

Bat daughter of

Bat Mitzvah celebration of a daughter's taking on the responsibility of being an adult Jew

Batyah midrashic name for Pharaoh's daughter

B'nei B'rak town in both ancient and modern Israel

Bimah lit. raised place; focal point of synagogue

B'rachah, pl. b'rachot blessing(s)

Bundist a member of the Bund, a Jewish socialist party founded in Russia in 1897

Chag ha'Aviv Festival of Spring; one of the names of Passover

Challah traditional braided egg bread used as part of Shabbat celebration

Chameitz leaven; traditionally, all leavened grain, wheat, spelt, barley and rye and derivatives that are forbidden during the eight day celebration of Passover

Charoset a mixture of wine, fruit, nuts and spices, symbolizing the mortar with which the Israelites made bricks during slavery

Cheider lit. room; traditional religious school

Conversos Jews who practiced Judaism secretly after converting to Christianity during the Spanish Inquisition

Dayeinu lit. it would have been enough

Haggadah pl. Haggadot, lit. telling; liturgy of the Passover seder

Halachah Jewish law

Hallel lit. praise; liturgy from Psalms added to morning prayers on holidays

Havdalah the prayer that marks the distinction between Shabbat or holidays and the rest of the week

Higia z'man the time has come

Kabbalists practitioners of Kabbalah, the Jewish mystical tradition

Kaddish from the root k-d-sh, to sanctify or set apart; prayer of praise, honor, or memory

Kaddish D'rabanan lit. the Scholars' Praise; traditionally, prayer said after study

Karpas a vegetable dipped in salt water during the seder

Ketubah traditional marriage document

Kibbutzim and moshavim collective agricultural settlements in Israel

Kiddush blessing said over wine or grape juice on sacred occasions

Kotel the remaining segment of the western retaining wall of the Temple in Jerusalem

L'chi lach lit. go for yourself (feminine), based on the biblical verse where God tells Abraham to leave his home and go to Canaan (GENESIS 12:1-2).

Maggid lit. telling; the section of the Haggadah containing the story of the Exodus

Makom kadosh lit. holy place

Manna food that sustained the Israelites in the desert

Maror bitter herbs

Matzah, pl. matzot unleavened bread eaten at Passover

M'chitzah divider between men's and women's sections in traditional synagogues

Me'ot Chittin lit. wheat money; charity collected before Passover to provide holiday food for the poor

Mikvah traditional Jewish ritual bath

Midrashic of, or pertaining to midrashim

Midrashim elaborations or interpretations of Biblical text (plural of midrash)

Mi Shebeirach lit. the one who blessed; blessing recited on one's behalf for different circumstances, including illness

Mishnah legal codification containing the core of the Oral Law

Mitzrayim lit. the narrows; Egypt

Mitzvah, pl. mitzvot lit. commandment; Jewish laws traditionally understood as God's word; also interpreted as opportunity to increase holiness

Moroteinu our teachers (female)

Moshe Hebrew for Moses

Niggun wordless melody

Nisan the Hebrew month in which Passover falls; the first seder is celebrated on the eve of the fifteenth of Nisan

Omer a biblically-ordained grain offering given on the second day of Passover from which we count seven weeks until the holiday of Shavuot

Partisans fighters in the underground resistance movement and guerilla war against the Nazis in World War II

Rabbanit, Rebbetzin, rabbi's wife, or, in contemporary usage, female rabbi

Raboteinu our rabbis

Rosh Chodesh lit. the head of the month; the first day of the Hebrew month when the new moon appears; a time that has traditionally been a semi-holiday for women

Sarai wife of Abram; when God makes the covenant with Abram, Sarai becomes Sarah and Abram becomes Abraham to reflect their changed status as matriarch and patriarch of the Israelite people (GENESIS 17:4)

Seder pl. s'darim lit. order; ordered readings and meal at Passover

Sefer Torah scroll of the Five Books of Moses

Sephardi pertaining to Jews from the Eastern Mediterranean, the Middle East, Caucasus and Central Asia, India, North Africa, and the Maghreb

Shabbat lit. rest; Sabbath

Sh'chinah lit. dwelling or indwelling presence; Divine Presence, often understood as the feminine manifestation of God.

Sh'ma central prayer in daily liturgy: "Hear O Israel, God is our God, God is One"

Sh'tei f'amim lit. two times

Talmud compilation of Mishnah and Gemara (commentary and supplement to Mishnah)

Tikkun Olam lit. repair of the world

Techine pl. techines women's Yiddish prayers, some of which were written by women, from the 16-19TH centuries in Eastern and Central Europe

Torah broadly, Jewish law and learning; specifically, the first five books of the Bible

Tzedakah lit. justice work; charity

Yah Sh'chinah two names of God linked together

Y'rushalayim Jerusalem

Z'man cheruteinu lit. our season of freedom; one of the names of Passover

Sources

p. 5 Introduction by Tamara Cohen, includes excerpts from 1997 Introduction by Sue Levi Elwell. Blessings section includes insights of Rachel Adler in Elwell, Sue Levi, ed. *And We Were All There: A Feminist Passover Haggadah.* Los Angeles: American Jewish Congress Feminist Center, 1994.

p. 10 Invocation for women's seders by Tamara Cohen, based on a prayer by Rav Alexandri, Babylonian Talmud Tractate Brachot 17a

p. 14 E-mail sent by Susannah Heschel April 5, 2001.

p. 22 *B'ruchot Habaot*, Music and lyrics by Debbie Friedman ©1988 Deborah Lynn Friedman (ASCAP), Sounds Write Productions, Inc. (ASCAP)

p. 23 *Makom Kadosh*/The Time is Now, Music by Debbie Friedman lyrics by Debbie Friedman and Tamara Cohen ©1996 Deborah Lynn Friedman (ASCAP), Sounds Write Productions, Inc. (ASCAP)

p. 24 Light These Lights, Music and lyrics by Debbie Friedman ©1995 Deborah Lynn Friedman (ASCAP), Sounds Write Productions, Inc. (ASCAP)

p. 26 Candlelighting blessing for women's seders by Tamara Cohen, Erika Katske and Susan Sapiro.

p. 27 *Techine* for candle lighting adapted by Nurit Shein and Sue Levi Elwell from a traditional Sephardic *techine* found in Cohen, Jonathan, ed. *The Sephardi Haggadah.* Jerusalem: Feldheim Publishers, 1988. For more on *techines* see Chava Weissler, *Voices of the Matriarchs.* Boston: Beacon, 1998.

pp. 29-30 *Kos Miryam* based on ©1992 Kol Ishah, PO Box 132, Wayland MA, 01778. May be used, but not sold, by notifying Kol Ishah in writing. Please include this copyright on all copies.

p. 31 The Journey Song, Music by Debbie Friedman lyrics by Debbie Friedman and Tamara Ruth Cohen ©1995 Deborah Lynn Friedman (ASCAP), Sounds Write Productions, Inc. (ASCAP)

p. 32 The Journey to Freedom by Tamara Cohen

pp. 35-36, 78, 100, 108 Four Cup introductions by Erika Katske and Susan Sapiro

p. 43 *Urchatz* by Erika Katske and Tamara Cohen

p. 45 *Karpas* by Ronnie M. Horn

p. 48 *Yachatz* by Tamara Cohen

p. 49 *Mi Shebeirach*, Music by Debbie Friedman lyrics by Debbie Friedman and D'rora Setel ©1988 Deborah Lynn Friedman (ASCAP), Sounds Write Productions, Inc. (ASCAP)

p. 51 *Ha Lachma Anya* by Tamara Cohen

p. 54 The Four Questions by Ronnie M. Horn

p. 56 *Avadim Hayinu* by Tamara Cohen, Erika Katske and Susan Sapiro

p. 59 *Ma'aseh* by Ronnie M. Horn

p. 60 *Kadish D'rabanan*, Music and lyrics by Debbie Friedman ©1988 Deborah Lynn Friedman (ASCAP), Sounds Write Productions, Inc. (ASCAP)

p. 61 The Four Daughters by Tamara Cohen, Sue Levi Elwell and Ronnie Horn

p. 63 *L'chi Lach* Music by Debbie Friedman lyrics by © Debbie Friedman and Savina Teubal, based on Genesis 12:1-2 ©1988 Deborah Lynn Friedman (ASCAP), Sounds Write Productions, Inc. (ASCAP)

p. 64 *Mit'chila* by Ronnie M. Horn

p. 65 *V'hi She'amda* by Tamara Cohen, Erika Katske and Susan Sapiro

p. 67 *Tz'i Ul'madi* by Tamara Cohen

p. 69 The Ten Plagues by Tamara Cohen

p. 71 Miriam's Song, Music and lyrics by Debbie Friedman, based on Exodus 15:20-21 ©1988 Deborah Lynn Friedman (ASCAP), Sounds Write Productions, Inc. (ASCAP)

p. 72 *Dayeinu* by Tamara Cohen

p. 74 *Pesach, Matzah, Maror* by Tamara Cohen, Sue Levi Elwell and Ronnie M. Horn

p. 75 *B'chol Dor Vador*, Music by Debbie Friedman, lyrics adapted from the Haggadah ©1996 Deborah Lynn Friedman (ASCAP), Sounds Write Productions, Inc. (ASCAP)

p. 77 *Hallel* by Tamara Cohen

p. 86 *Maror* by Tamara Cohen, Pappenheim quote from Daniel Boyarin, *Unheroic Conduct.* Berkeley, University of California Press, 1997, p. 180. Szold quote from *Daughter of Zion: Henrietta Szold and American Jewish Womanhood.* Jewish Historical Society of Maryland. 1995, p. 71.

p. 92 *Tzafun* by Ronnie M. Horn

p. 95 *Bareich* reading by Susan Sapiro

p. 97 *Birkat Hamazon*, Music by Debbie Friedman, lyrics by Debbie Friedman based on traditional text ©1996 Deborah Lynn Friedman (ASCAP), Sounds Write Productions, Inc. (ASCAP)

p. 101 *Sh'foch Chamatcha* by Ronnie M. Horn

p. 102 *Mir'yam Han'viah* ©1989 Leila Gal Berner. Conceived by Rabbi Leila Gal Berner and Rabbi Arthur Waskow; Hebrew by Leila Gal Berner. This song originally appeared in *Or Chadash*, a Shabbat morning siddur published by P'nai Or Religious Fellowship. Used by permission of author.

p. 110 *Nirtzah* by Tamara Cohen

p. 111 Jerusalem by Tamara Cohen

p. 112 *T'fillat Haderech*, Music by Debbie Friedman lyrics by Debbie Friedman, based on traditional text ©1998 Deborah Lynn Friedman (ASCAP), Sounds Write Productions, Inc. (ASCAP)

p. 113 B'irkat Hamzon is taken from *A Kolot Egalitarian Bentcher*, published by Kolot: The Center for Jewish Women's and Gender Studies. The Hebrew was adapted by Reena Kling and Miriam Bronstein for a bentcher they developed for Havurat Shalom in Boston. The English translation of the Birkat Hamazon from *Kol Haneshamah: Nashir Unevareh* is used by permission of The Reconstructionist Press, 7804 Montgomery Ave. Suite #9, Elkins Park, PA 19027-2649 fax 215. 782. 8805 e-mail press@jrf.org.

p. 122-123 *Orah Hi* by Rabbi Jill Hammer

p. 136-137 Glossary compiled by Susan Sapiro

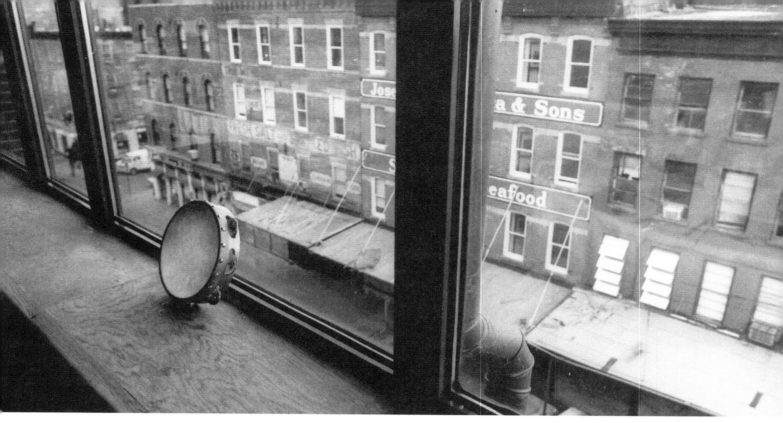

THE JOURNEY CONTINUES

©2006 Ma'yan: The Jewish Women's Project.

Updated and edited by Tamara Cohen.

Aside from the many editors, writers and committee members listed in the Acknowledgements, the following people have also helped Ma'yan with this Haggadah over the years: Joyce Antler, Esther Ann Asch, Kathy Barr, Ayelet Cohen, Coraline Dahlin, Rachel Dobkin, Shirley Frank, Randee Friedman, Gwynn Kessler, Benay Lappe, Paulette Lipton, Nurit Shein, Rabbi David Sulomm Stein.

This Haggadah is a publication of Ma'yan: The Jewish Women's Project, a program of the Jewish Community Center in Manhattan. A companion cassette/CD recorded by Debbie Friedman and a songbook are available through Sounds Write Productions, Inc.

contact: Sounds Write Productions
6685 Norman Lane, San Diego, CA 92120
tel. 619. 697. 6120 fax. 619. 697. 6124

photo credits

Ma'yan is indebted to the generosity of Beth Shepherd Peters and Joan Roth who have donated their beautiful photography.

Beth Shepherd Peters
cover (top right and left, bottom right), pp. 2-3, 17, 19, 21, 23, 27, 31-35, 38, 43, 45-46, 48, 50, 52, 53 (right), 54-55, 61 (middle,bottom), 62-65, 67, 69, 71, 74, 80-83, 85-86, 88-89, 90 (middle, bottom right), 91 (right), 92, 96, 103-104, 110, 112 (bottom), 128.

Joan Roth
pp. 20, 24, 44, 49, 59-60, 61 (top), 68, 76, 79, 87, 94, 98, 109, 111.

p. 47 Jews for Racial and Economic Justice; p. 53 (left) Mia N. Johnson; pp. 58, Tamara Cohen; p. 63 (bottom right) Nisan Young Women Leaders; p. 66 Courtesy of International Ladies Garment Workers Union, Kheel Center for Labor-Management Documentation and Archives, Cornell University; p. 73 Debbie Cooper; p. 75 Ayelet Cohen; p. 78 Rose Schneiderman photo courtesy of Brown Brothers; p. 90, clockwise from top left, Congregation Beth Torah, Susan Woog Wagner, DC Jewish Community Center, Mary Anne Winig, Jewish Federation of Greater Kansas City; p. 91 Seder plate by Amy Klein Reichert; p. 93 DC Jewish Community Center; p. 97 Ruth Silverman; p. 99 15th century Italian Haggadah, Schocken Library, Jerusalem, Israel; p. 102 Project Kesher; p. 106 Omer tapestry by Anika Soffer, designed by Georges Goldstein, photo by Paulette Lipton.

Miriam's cups

All photos of cups are Miriam's Cups made for "Drawing From the Source: Miriam, Women's Creativity and New Ritual," an invitational exhibition created by Ma'yan and held at Hebrew Union College-Jewish Institute of Religion, March 16-April 30, 1997.

cover and p. 77 Dalya Luttwak; p. 22 Elee Koplow; p. 29 Susan Duhan Felix; p. 30 Kathy Hart; p. 36 Judy Sirota Rosenthal; p. 41 Kathlean Levine Gahagan; p. 42 Avigayil (Andra Ellis); p. 57 Beth Grossman; p. 70 Tania Kravath; p. 78 Linda Leviton; p.100 Linda Gissen; p. 101 Grace Bakst Wapner; p. 108 Yael Brotman; p. 112 Norma Minkowitz.

For more information about Ma'yan and resources for other holiday rituals and women's programming for your community, contact:

Ma'yan: The Jewish Women's Project
The JCC in Manhattan
334 Amsterdam Ave.
New York, NY 10023

tel. 646. 505. 4440 fax. 646. 505. 4448
email. infomayan@mayan.org website. www.mayan.org